HAPPINESS IS A CHOICE YOU MAKE

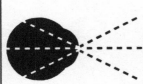

HAPPINESS IS A CHOICE YOU MAKE

LESSONS FROM A YEAR AMONG THE OLDEST OLD

JOHN LELAND

THORNDIKE PRESS
A part of Gale, a Cengage Company

A Cengage Company

Farmington Hills, Mich • San Francisco • New York • Waterville, Maine
Meriden, Conn • Mason, Ohio • Chicago

Copyright © 2018 John Leland.
Grateful acknowledgment is made to Jonas Mekas for permission to reprint an excerpt from his poem "Old Is This Rushing of Rain" from *Idylls of Semeniskia*. Translated from the Lithuanian by the author's brother, Adolfas Mekas. Copyright © Hallelujah Editions, 2007.
Thorndike Press, a part of Gale, a Cengage Company.

ALL RIGHTS RESERVED
Thorndike Press® Large Print Popular and Nonfiction.
The text of this Large Print edition is unabridged.
Other aspects of the book may vary from the original edition.
Set in 16 pt. Plantin.

LIBRARY OF CONGRESS CIP DATA ON FILE.
CATALOGUING IN PUBLICATION FOR THIS BOOK
IS AVAILABLE FROM THE LIBRARY OF CONGRESS

ISBN-13: 978-1-4328-4581-0 (hardcover)

Published in 2018 by arrangement with Sarah Crichton Books, an imprint of Farrar, Straus and Giroux.

Printed in Mexico
2 3 4 5 6 7 22 21 20 19 18

For Mom, maker of swans,
with love and gratitude

Aging is an extraordinary process whereby you become the person you always should have been.

— David Bowie

CONTENTS

CONTENTS

■ ■ ■ ■

PART I
MEET THE ELDERS

■ ■ ■ ■

ONE:
SURPRISE OF A LIFETIME
"GET ME A GIN!"

"Do you know what you want to do when you get old?"

After a year of answering questions, John Sorensen asked one of his own. We were in the kitchen of his apartment on Manhattan's Upper West Side, where he had lived for forty-eight years, the last six of them alone, since the death of his longtime partner. Around him was a mural of trees he had painted years earlier, with branches stretching up to the ceiling. Thanksgiving was approaching, John's favorite day of the year, when he left the apartment to be among friends. But this year, 2015, he didn't think he would be well enough to go. The kitchen looked exactly as it had on my last visit and the one before, because John made sure nothing was ever changed — he was losing his eyesight, and he feared that if anything was moved he wouldn't be able to find it. On the small TV and VCR by the

13

refrigerator he was getting ready to watch *Seven Brides for Seven Brothers,* which always cheered him up. He knew the movie so well that he didn't need to see the screen.

We were talking about the things in John's life that gave him pleasure. It took a little prompting, because John always began on the dark side, and it wasn't a visit unless he said he wanted to die. Yet once he got going, his mood always brightened.

"I played the second act of *Parsifal* recently, with Jonas Kaufmann," he said, wrapping himself in the memory. "The most beautiful tenor I've ever heard. Very romantic-looking. The first time I saw him was after Walter died. He was singing and my God he was good."

John, who was ninety-one at the time, was one of six strangers I began visiting at the start of 2015 who unexpectedly changed my life. I'm sure none of them intended to play that role. I met them while reporting a newspaper series called "85 & Up," in which I set out to follow six older New Yorkers for a year.

It began, as all stories do, with a search for characters. I met them at senior centers and in nursing homes, through home care agencies or their personal web pages. Some were still working; some never left the

14

house. I met abiding Communists and mah-jongg players and Holocaust survivors and working artists and a ninety-six-year-old lesbian metalworker who still organized tea dances. All had lost something: mobility, vision, hearing, spouses, children, peers, memory. But few had lost everything. They belonged to one of the fastest-growing age groups in America, now so populous that they had their own name: the oldest old.

I, too, had lost some things. My marriage had come apart after nearly three decades, and I was living alone for the first time. I was fifty-five years old, with a new girlfriend and new questions about my place in the world: about age, about love and sex and fatherhood, about work and satisfaction.

I was also the main caregiver for my eighty-six-year-old mother, who moved from her ranch house in New Jersey to an apartment building for seniors in Lower Manhattan after my father's death. It was not a role I performed with much distinction. I did my best to have dinner with her every couple of weeks and accompanied her on the occasional night in the ER. I pretended not to notice that she might want more than that — best to honor her independence, I told myself — and so did she. Neither of us was well equipped for the

15

stage of life we had stumbled into together: she, at eighty-six, without an idea of where to find meaning, and me without an idea of how to help. But there we were.

One of the first people I interviewed for the series was a woman named Jean Goldberg, 101, a former secretary at Crayola, who began our conversation by shouting "Get me a gin!" and then proceeded to tell the story of the man who did her wrong — seventy years in the past, but still as near as anything in her life. She was in a wheelchair in a nursing home, but she had lived in her own apartment until she was 100, when she had a series of falls and no longer felt safe on her own. After a great first meeting, she asked to postpone our second interview because she was not feeling well; by the time the new date arrived, she was gone. Whatever strategies she had devised to take her to age 101 — humor, I think, but also a stubborn refusal to yield, even when it cost her — were gone with her.

Each person had a story to tell — about their family lives during the Great Depression or their sex lives during the Second World War, about participating in the civil rights movement or being told by their parents that they weren't "college material." But mainly I was interested in what their lives were like now, from the moment they got up until they went to bed. How did they get through the day, and what were their hopes for the morrow? How did they manage their medications, their children, and their changing bodies, which were now reversing the trajectory of childhood, losing capabilities as fast as they had once gained them? Was there a threshold at which life was no longer worth living?

Their qualifications as experts were simply that they were living it. As the British novelist Penelope Lively, then eighty, put it, "One of the few advantages of age is that you can report on it with a certain authority; you are a native now, and know what goes on here. . . . Our experience is one unknown to most of humanity, over time. We are the pioneers." I joined them in their homes, on trips to the doctor, in the hospital, in jazz clubs and bars and a beach house on the Jersey shore. I met their children, their lovers, doctors, home attendants, friends, and a former district attorney who had prosecuted one for obscenity long ago, and who now wanted to apologize. When one suddenly disappeared, his phone disconnected, I tracked him through Brooklyn's hospital system, where he was having parts of two toes amputated. I listened and learned.

Gradually I noticed something quite unexpected happening. Every visit, no matter how dark the conversation got — and some days it got quite morbid — raised my spirits like no other work I have ever done. I expected the year to bring great changes in them. I didn't expect it to change me.

The six became my surrogate elders: warm, cranky, demanding, forgetful, funny, sage, repetitive, and sometimes just too weary to talk. They chided me for not visiting enough and fed me chocolates or sent me clippings to read. I changed lightbulbs in their apartments and nodded sympathetically about Israel and told them about my relationship with my mother. Often they were admirable. They held grudges and devised Rube Goldberg–type systems for remembering to take their medications — foolproof as long as they didn't drop the little white heart pills, which were too small for their fingers and invisible on the floor.

With them I had to give up the idea that I knew about life. It was a humbling experience, but also an energizing one. I didn't have to be the expert or critic, challenging the things they told me. Instead I let them guide me through the world as they saw it. I gained the most from accepting ideas that my instincts told me to reject. My instincts thought they knew what it was like to be ninety, but they didn't, and as soon as I quieted them, the learning got a lot easier. Being an expert is exhausting. Being a student — letting go of your ego — is like sitting for a banquet at the best restaurant you'll ever visit.

Like all good literary characters, each of the elders wanted something — as did I, even if I didn't know it at first.

The six I finally chose came from different backgrounds and social strata. Frederick Jones, who was eighty-seven when I met him, was a World War II vet and retired civil servant with a dirty mind and a weak heart, which had kept him in a hospital or rehab center for much of the previous year. The first time we met, he told me about picking up a woman thirty years younger than he in a department store; he couldn't remember which. Fred was a player, no less so now that the equipment was in retirement. Old photos in his apartment showed him in sharp suits and with a burly mustache, but by the time I met him he was embarrassed to go to church in his orthopedic shoes, so he spent most of his days in an unkempt apartment atop three flights of stairs that he could barely manage. Fred had his own ideas about what it meant to be old. He asked God for 110 years, and he never doubted that he would get them. He started every day, he said, by giving thanks for another sunrise. When I asked him what was the happiest period of his life, he did not hesitate. "Right now," he said. He was the first to cheer me up.

Helen Moses, age ninety, found the second love of her life in a Bronx nursing home, against gale-force resistance from her daughter. The romance had been going for six years by the time I met them.

"I love Howie," she said, gazing at Howie Zeimer, who lived down the hall.

"Same goes for me, too," Howie said. He was in a wheelchair by the side of her bed, holding her hand. "You're the one woman in my lifetime, I mean it."

"I can't hear you," she said, "but it better be good."

John Sorensen lost most of his interest in life after the death of his lover of sixty years, a bookseller named Walter Caron. "You won't get much wisdom from me," John said the first time we met. "I know a little bit about a lot of things." We talked about opera and Fire Island (price of his beach house in 1960: ten grand), and about John's frustration that he couldn't do the things he used to. He had gladly nursed Walter in his decline, but now he couldn't forgive his own failing body. He refused to use a walker or wheelchair, because he found them unsightly, so he never went out. His knuckles, swollen from gout, resembled mismatched drawer knobs, and were about as pliant. Yet talking always cheered him up, even talking about his wish to die. He exercised every day and seemed to take morbid pride that his body insisted on keeping on. "Honey, I'm so much better off than so many people, I know it," he said. "Still, I've had it. I'm not unhappy, but I'll be glad when it's over." The only bad thing about dying, John said, "is that I won't be alive long enough to enjoy the fact that I finally died."

Ping Wong, eighty-nine, had lucked into the sweet spot in the social safety net: she paid two hundred dollars a month for a subsidized apartment near Gramercy Park, and had a home attendant seven days a week, for seven hours a day, paid for by Medicaid. Old age, she said, was less stressful than working or caring for her husband, which had worn her out. Yet she missed her late husband and the son who was murdered in China. "I try not to think about bad things," she said. "It's not good for old people to complain."

Ruth Willig, by contrast, was quick to say she was unhappy with her life, but then upset to read that characterization in the paper — that wasn't her. Over the year, I came to see Ruth's complaints as a way of asserting some leverage on her life, rather than passively accepting what came her way. Shortly before I met her, she had been forced to move from her high-priced assisted living facility in Park Slope, Brooklyn, when the owner decided to sell it for higher-priced condos. She had given up her car, her privacy, her ability to keep her own schedule just to move there. Now, five years older and less mobile, she had lost that home as well, and the friends she had made there. So at ninety-one she was starting over at another assisted living center in a more remote part of Brooklyn, Sheepshead Bay. She was among strangers, in an unfamiliar neighborhood far from her nearest daughter.

"Someone here called me a feisty old lady," she said one morning. "She didn't say 'old lady.' She said 'feisty lady.' I'm putting in the 'old.' I don't give up easily. Maybe that's what it is. I really push."

A March snow had blanketed the streets outside, which meant another day she wouldn't be going out. "I know what I am, I'm ninety-one, I tell everyone," she said.

"I'm not afraid of it. I'm kind of proud of it, compared to some of the others who have so many disabilities. I'm very lucky. I try to be healthy. I think about how I'll die. But I just keep myself busy with reading books and reading the paper. Try to make myself happy, but that's not so easy. I wish I'd be happier."

And Jonas Mekas, the filmmaker and writer, at ninety-two had the energy and urgency of three thirty-year-olds. He was still making movies, compiling memoirs and scrapbooks, raising money for his nonprofit organization, and running his website.

One day he sent me an unpublished poem he had written in 2005.

I worked all my life to become young
no, you can't persuade me to get old
I will die twenty-seven

His friends were younger than I. Far from slowing down, he was speeding up, he said, because now he could work exclusively on his own projects.

Those were my six teachers for a year. They were dying, of course, as we all are, and they were close enough to the end to consider not just the fact of death but the form it would take. Death had lost its abstraction. Would they keep their cognitive faculties? Would their last days drag out? Tomorrow might bring a fall, a broken hip, a stroke, a black hole where they once stored the name of the person they were talking to. Every time a phone call went unanswered I worried. Within eighteen months, two of them had died.

Discussions about the elderly tend to focus on the very real problems of old age, like the declines in the body and mind, or the billions of dollars spent on end-of-life medical care. Or else they single out that remarkable old lady who seems to defy aging altogether, drinking martinis and running marathons in her nineties. This vision is particularly seductive to baby boomers, with its promise that you, too, can master the secrets of "successful aging." All you have to do is basically extend late middle age — join a club, volunteer, exercise, fall in love, learn Italian, don't get sick. Did I mention don't get sick? Good luck with that, hope it works out for you.

The elders I spent time with, like the vast majority of older people, didn't fit either of these story lines. They lived with loss and disability but did not define themselves by it, and got up each morning with wants and needs, no less so because their knees hurt or they couldn't do the crossword puzzle like they used to. Old age wasn't something that hit them one day when they weren't careful. It also wasn't a problem to be fixed. It was a stage of life like any other, one in which they were still making decisions about how they wanted to live, still learning about themselves and the world.

Until recently, relatively few people experienced this stage, and even fewer reached it in good health. But that has changed. More people are living past age eighty-five than at any time in human history (nearly six million in America, up from under a million in 1960), and they are living longer once they get there. Which means that your parents are the vanguard that your kids think they are. An American who turns eighty-five in 2018 was born with a life expectancy of less than sixty years. That's a lot of time not planned for, and a lot of old people who know something about living long.

Mostly we think of this as a cause for worry rather than a resource to be tapped. So much loneliness and isolation, so many wrinkles. In movies, beauty is always young, and amorous elders are dirty old men. We like people to ride into the sunset when their mission is complete. How much more exciting if Thelma and Louise, instead of driving off a cliff, got old and started a mentoring program in downtown Denver, sometimes taking male companions, raising heck along with their home attendants? But old people don't get to tell these stories. As May Sarton wrote, in her novel *As We Are Now,* published when she was sixty-one, "The trouble is, old age is not interesting until one gets there. It's a foreign country with an unknown language to the young and even to the middle-aged." Pretty smart for someone only sixty-one.

Consider how we address old people: sweetie, dear, good girl, young man. Aren't they cute? And how are *we* today, Mrs. Johnson? Ninety-two years young? Bless your heart. A wise old person is someone who uses Instagram like a teenager. For most of history, societies turned to their oldest members for wisdom. Children watched their grandparents get old and die in the family home. But the same technology that made it possible for more people to survive to old age has also devalued their knowledge of the world. Old people often inhabit a world of their own, not particularly pleasant to visit. In one study, people over sixty said fewer than one-quarter of the people with whom they discussed "important matters" were under thirty-six; if you exclude relatives, it dropped to 6 percent. An analysis by the gerontologist Karl Pillemer of Cornell found that Americans are more likely to have friends of another race than friends who are more than ten years apart from them in age.

Pillemer said his life was changed when he stopped thinking about old people as a problem and started to think of them as an asset, a repository of wisdom and experience. The title of this book comes from one of the first lessons the elders taught me: that even as our various faculties decline, we still wield extraordinary influence over the quality of our lives. As Ping put it, "When you're old, you have to make yourself happy. Otherwise you get older." The six all found a level of happiness not in their external circumstances, but in something they carried with them. No one wants to lose his partner of sixty years, or to give up walking because it hurts too much, but we have some choice in how we process the loss and the life left to us. We can focus on what we've lost or on the life we have now. Health factors, as shattering as they can be, are only part of the story.

So there's a choice, maybe. Take the blue pill and you're bemoaning life without the sharp memory or the job that once made you special; take the red pill and you're giving thanks for a life that still includes people you love. You can go to a museum and think, I'm confined to a wheelchair in a group of half-deaf old people. Or you can think, Matisse!

The more time I spent with the elders, the more I thought about how to get there now — how to choose happiness amid all the other options. The answer, I began to realize, was one that ran counter to all my expectations. If you want to be happy, learn to think like an old person.

The good news about getting old is that there is good news. Older people report a greater sense of well-being and fewer negative emotions than younger people. That sense of well-being rises until sometime in the seventh decade, then begins a gradual decline, but still remains higher at ninety than at twenty. As much as we idealize adolescence and young adulthood, older people are more content, less anxious or fearful, less afraid of death, more likely to see the good side of things and accept the bad, than young adults. As Henry Miller — nobody's idea of a Pollyanna — wrote, "At eighty I believe I am a far more cheerful person than I was at twenty or thirty. I most definitely would not want to be a teenager again. Youth may be glorious, but it is also painful to endure." Experience helps older people moderate their expectations and makes them more resilient when things don't go as hoped. When they do have negative experiences, they don't dwell on them as much as younger people do. Researchers call this the positivity effect. It's a puzzle: How can people whose minds and bodies are in decline — whose best years, as we have come to think of them, are receding into the past — feel better about their lives than people with the world in front of them? Don't they know their lives are shot?

Or: What do they know that the rest of us don't?

The six elders all developed their own mechanisms for getting through the day, but their strategies often boiled down to the same thing: spend your dwindling time and energy on the things you can still do that give you satisfaction, not on lamenting those you once did but now can't. Gerontologists call this "selective optimization with compensation": older people make the most of what they have left and compensate for what they have lost. (James Brown called this "She Got to Use What She Got to Get What

She Wants.") If you have 30 percent of your former capacity, use it on things you love. An arrogance of youth, perhaps, is to think that life isn't worth living once you can't do the things you do now.

In chess, players sometimes use a technique called retrograde analysis to strengthen their midgame play. Instead of working forward from the beginning of a game, they work backward from an endgame, figuring out the sequence of moves that led to a particular arrangement of pieces. If white has a slight edge, what move did he or she make to get there, and what move before that one? And so on. The idea is that at the start of a game, each player has so many pieces on the board and potential ways to move them that it is very difficult to see which moves might lead to a desired result, but if you work backward from a destination, the choices become fewer and less opaque. You can ignore the moves that don't get you where you want to go and focus on the ones that do.

As an exercise, imagine what it means to have a good life at seventy-five, eighty, or eighty-five. An American man turning eighty-five has a life expectancy of six years; a woman can expect to live another seven. That's almost as long as adolescence. What do you want your life to be like then — what pleasures, what rewards, what daily activities and human connections? Now work your way backward to see what moves will lead you there — which pieces and positions are important, which can be sacrificed along the way.

The first step is to imagine what a good life is at that age. This may not be easy. Most of us don't spend a lot of time with very old people, and when we do, it's usually about trying to help with their problems, not asking them what makes them happy or fulfilled. But if you start with the idea that you will someday be old, and not broken down from a life of physical labor, what do you want those years to look like? Chances are you'll be in better shape than your ancestors, who were lucky to live past seventy — better educated, with more money and better health. You might want to be intellectually stimulated or emotionally supported by family members. You might want a loving life partner, or memories of a happy marriage. You might want music or art, or contact with young people, or to be productive and useful even as your body declines. There will be limits, of course. At age eighty-five and older, 72 percent of people have at least one disability, and 55 percent have more than one. So you might not want to make love in the pounding surf at Waikiki or go live off the grid. How do you imagine a good life with a body that doesn't do all the things it used to?

Now think of the steps that will get you there. Fortunately, most are things that make us happier and more fulfilled throughout our lives. If you want close, supportive relationships with friends and family members when you're eighty-five, trace a series of moves leading up to that, all the way back to the present time. Pleasant, right? That's the universe telling you to spend more time with people you care about. If you want a life of purpose, don't you think you'd better start finding your purpose now? You may not get there by working more hours, coming home late, putting off time with your friends and family. Maybe you want a different job, a long talk with your son, a move to a different part of the country. Maybe the answer is ending a marriage in which you're no longer helping each other grow. I never said this was going to be easy.

A benefit of trying to imagine a good life at eighty-five is that it means viewing old age not as a postscript tacked onto an already complete story but as a continuation. It means seeing your life course differently: not as a series of milestones you pass at different ages — finding a job, moving into your first home, et cetera — but as a long composition in which motifs repeat and develop over decades. Instead of assigning education, work, or romance to particular times of our lives, we might keep revisiting them in different variations throughout that span. They add up, first as experiences, later as memories. By the end you're living in all of that music at once.

Each of the six elders practiced happiness differently, some more habitually than others. Fred gave thanks for each day, even though objectively those days looked pretty hard. Ruth had her children and extended family, for whom she had become the glue holding the others together. Jonas had his work, which he never distinguished from his life. He didn't take vacations or knock off work at the end of a hard day. He sought good company and good food and wine, onscreen and in his life. "I don't leave any space for depression to come in," he said. "I gravitate more to neutral areas or to positive activities. I'm not interested to film some dark, depressive aspects. I'm more interested in where people come together, they're singing and dancing, more happy aspects. Why? It's my nature. I consider that maybe unconsciously I'm thinking that's what humanity needs more."

Ping had daily games of mah-jongg with women in her building, and Helen had Howie. Even John, despite his wish to die, spent most of his time reliving memories of a happy life. Nearly blind and barely able to feed himself, he willed himself back to better times, in vivid color and detail. Often he surprised me. "It was one of those God-given days, where everything just glowed," he said one day. "I remember the ocean was calm, and it just glittered like diamonds out there. At the end of the day my brother was visiting me, and I have pictures of the last time I saw him alive." Each of the six was showing me ways to stop stewing in life's problems. But first they had to teach me to pay attention.

My seventh teacher in this master class was my mother, Dorothy, who lives in a senior building in Lower Manhattan and gets around in a motorized wheelchair. "If you want to know what it's like to get old," she said recently, "it stinks." When my father died in 2004, she realized that she didn't own a pair of boots, because he had always driven her to the door of wherever they went. Preparing for eventualities — for example, being eighty-six — was never her first priority. "I never thought about it," she said. "I'm not giving you very good answers." Since 2011, when she nearly died following an operation on her spine, she has expressed only one strong wish in life, and that is to die. She still blames my younger brother, Joe, for not letting her die.

I was on assignment in Iraq at the time, so Joe, who lives in North Carolina, was the one on the front lines. The operation was to fuse two vertebrae, and we had discouraged it or asked her to delay it until I was back in New York. She'd already had one spinal fusion operation, a few years earlier, and it had knocked her out for months and brought little relief. But she was in a lot of pain and decided to go forward.

For the second operation she was older and weaker, and when an infection flared up her body put up little resistance. The doctors wanted approval to insert a feeding tube to get her through the infection. She had left us a Do Not Resuscitate order, so my brother and I consulted over a garbled cell phone connection, losing each other in midsentence. This was a terrible way to decide the life or death of your mother. Her DNR said to withhold care if she had no reasonable chance of regaining a meaningful life. But this was more like bringing in a

35

hose if the drapes in her room caught fire. Afterward she would return to the life she had in her neat apartment. She had friends and grandchildren she loved; she had matinee concerts at the Philharmonic. People with much less enjoy great lives. It seemed ungrateful to reject that life as not worth living. If she wanted to starve to death, she could do it without our help. We approved the tube.

What do you say when your mother tells you she has no productive role left to play, or scolds her children for not having let her die? I mostly avoided this question for years, until I met John Sorensen. It was easier with someone who wasn't my parent. In our early meetings, when John said he hoped to die soon, I always said I hoped he wouldn't. The world would be a duller place without him. But over the year, John invited me to see his life from a different perspective. He had taken stock of the things he still enjoyed and weighed them against the effort it took to keep going. The rewards were becoming fewer and redundant; the effort was increasing. Surely they were his to weigh, not mine. By midyear I stopped saying I hoped he wouldn't die, and by winter I stopped thinking it. None of us really wants immortality on other people's terms; it's no kindness to

36

wish a scaled-down version of it on the people who want it least.

Then just before Christmas of 2015, near the end of my year among the elders, my mother was back in the hospital with chest pains and high levels of the enzyme troponin in her blood, evidence of a heart attack. My brother was due up from North Carolina in a day or two. Visions of DNRs danced in my head. Those first days, propped up in the hospital bed under the ghostly fluorescents, she was more at peace than I had seen her in years, telling me whom she wanted to perform the eulogy after her death. I should check out the minister's Facebook page, she said; it's all about sermons and jazz. Hooked up to beeping electronic monitors and tubes, she drifted in and out of consciousness, eyes placid behind smudged glasses. She mused about a recent bout with pneumonia, how pleasant it would have been to have just let it take her gently away. Now she was back at the threshold, or so she thought. It was the kind of exit she always said she wanted, nothing fancy or too painful, and with lots of nurses at her call.

So what had I learned? To see my mother through John's eyes was to see a life that had once had value to its owner but no longer did. She wanted to be relieved of it; she had carried it long enough. I wouldn't make her keep a scarf she no longer cared about. Isn't part of appreciating the value of a life being able to acknowledge when that value drops?

By the time my brother arrived from North Carolina, it was clear she was going to survive. No heroic measures necessary, no need for the DNR. The serenity she had shown in the face of death gave way to irritation at the hospital routine. When my brother and I compared notes, it was as if we had sat with different women. I believe the woman I visited was the happier one. Did I ever join her in wishing she would die? I think not, any more than I did with John. But I had begun to accept death as a natural element of old age — something we do, not something that happens to us. Quitting is no less noble than fighting; in the end, both turn out the same way.

I'm learning. I still have a ways to go. Wine helps. Get me a gin!

Growing up, I had little contact with older people. My grandparents had all died by the time I was three, and though my mother's aunt Dorothy came to visit every Christmas, she stopped when her health declined, so I never saw her as anything but the somewhat crusty former nurse who played a spirited "Alley Cat" on our upright piano. Later on I got to know my wife's grandfather, Al, a cigar smoker and former truck driver, whom I think of as the guy who broke his hip at age ninety jumping over the net after a tennis game, then ran away with a woman from the hospital and made it as far as St. Louis, where the car and the relationship broke down. I'm sure some of this is accurate. As for the rest, I don't want to know. He lived to be over one hundred, and died in an advanced state of dementia. Everybody had an Al story. At his memorial, a cousin said that Al thought the words "bar mitzvah" meant "the bar is open." The rabbi's theme was "Who knows what the morrow will bring?" which seemed ill-suited to the death of a frail centenarian in a nursing home. Everyone knew what his morrow would bring. My wife, who cared for him in his last years, said she hoped to get cancer and die before getting old. She considered taking up smoking.

At a recent dinner, my mother lamented that she'd never thought about a productive coda to her working years. "I spent one-quarter of my life as a student, learning," she said. "Then you spend half of your life in a productive capacity. Then you spend another twenty-five years doing nothing, being useless. A useless eater. I think our society must find something for these people to do."

Maybe the time to learn old age's lessons is in advance. The lessons are out there. Six million teachers are in it now. John Sorensen said he promised himself that when he got old he would shave every day and not drool, but at ninety-one he shaved occasionally and the muscles in his mouth were too slack to keep the saliva from running down his chin. A lesson of old age is that it's not what you think, and the debilities you thought defined people are often just more things you live with. We'd do ourselves a big favor not to be scared of growing old, but to embrace the mixed bag that the years have to offer, however severe the losses. A long-term survey of people in Ohio found that those who had positive perceptions of aging, measured by whether they agreed or disagreed with statements like "As you get older, you are less useful," went on to live an average of 7.5 years longer, a bigger boost than that associated with exercising or not smoking.

The elders all knew something you can't get on the Internet, which is how to be old,

40

and how the world looks from the perspective of someone who has lived in it for a while, and who will soon be leaving it. As Helen Moses often tells her daughter, "I was your age, but you were never my age." They are not, as they are often described these days, an "age tsunami" — something gathering out at sea that will soon wreak devastation on "our" shores. They are us — if not now, then someday. And if we are not willing to learn from them, we will miss important lessons about what it means to be human. Old age is the last thing we'll ever do, and it might teach us about how to live now.

I didn't know any of this when I started dropping in on the lives of the six elders. Mainly I hoped to show the pains and hardships of old age. Journalism loves problems. What else, I reasoned, was old age made of?

All I knew was that my life had been turned upside down, and the things I thought were solid had proved temporary. At least I wasn't old, I thought.

Two:
The Paradox of Old Age
"RIGHT NOW ARE YOU HAPPY?"

At first I found exactly what I was looking for. Old age was the gift that kept on taking. Ping's arthritic knees and shoulders hurt so much they kept her up at night. John was lonely and scared to leave his apartment, barely able to raise his arm to comb his hair. The gout in his fingers made it difficult even to feed himself — sometimes he just lowered his mouth to the plate to eat. Ruth lost her home and her friends and had stopped walking outside. Fred fell in his kitchen one night and couldn't get up, so he went to sleep on the floor until the morning. Each had the makings of a sad and moving tale. All I had to do was follow my preconceptions about old age.

"I hate it here," Helen said when I first visited her in the nursing home, in the Riverdale section of the Bronx. "I never thought I'd be in a nursing home. That's when nobody wants you."

All six saw their muscles wasting away, a condition known as sarcopenia that begins in all of us in middle age; by age eighty, people have lost about one-third to one-half of their muscle mass. The skin on their necks and arms hung slack and blotchy in places, as if retaining the ghosts of old bruises. Almost the first thing I noticed about Fred, shaking hands outside his apartment door, was that the thenar muscle at the base of his thumb, instead of bulging, was flat or concave. "See this?" he said, pinching the loose skin by his thumb. "The other day I had a cord where the two-way plug goes into the three-way socket, and I couldn't plug it in. I told a friend about it, and boom, he got it right away. I'd been pushing at it for days." Even Jonas, who was still traveling and making films, couldn't work the small buttons on the new video cameras, and his hand shook badly when he tried to write. Of the six, five needed a cane or walker to get around, which meant they had to rely on others to visit them. Simple mental tasks, like remembering a name or whether they took a pill, became challenges they often failed. None lived with a mate.

How hard was old age? On my second visit with Ruth, she described a routine trip to a doctor's office the day before. It was the tail end of winter and the city was blanketed in new snow and ice. She was still exhausted from the experience.

The first cab she called didn't come. Ruth is a compact woman used to doing things for herself, but since moving to the new facility she had become more sedentary and, like my mother, had gained a few pounds from the desserts offered at every meal. When the second cab came, it was an SUV, too high for her to climb into. Here was a dilemma of old age: whether to let the driver lift her into the cab — by the tush, she stressed — or to give up. Finally she managed to lean her upper body backward onto the seat and pull her legs in. A routine trip to the doctor became a whole day of stress.

"What do I look forward to?" she asked, pausing to think about it. She did not have an answer. "I find that I'm sad most of the time. I'm not happy anymore, and that bothers me." She was still angry about being forced to leave her old assisted living facility eight months earlier, "missing the people that I liked over there."

I asked whether she agreed with the research showing that old people are happier than young adults. "Not me," she said. "Not I." She ended the interview early because she was too tired to go on.

None of the six could say that tomorrow would be better than today. It promised more decline of their minds and bodies, less control over their lives, fewer friends and loved ones, a slow or fast progression toward death. Whatever health problems they had — diabetes, arthritis, memory loss, heart disease, weak vision or weak hearing — were only getting worse. Cuts healed slowly, and coughs took forever. They never saw people like themselves on television; strangers looked past them on the streets or in stores, not wanting to get entangled in the life of an old man or woman. And if they complained, well, they ran the risk that their children would shut them out.

Yet as I kept visiting, another story started to emerge. Helen said she appreciated her relationship with Howie in ways that she had not with her fifty-seven-year marriage, which had been loving but had started too young for any real courtship. "It's much more romantic with Howie," she said.

"You'll never understand." Ping said that despite her aches, life was easier now, with more leisure and less stress. "I never compare my happiness with the past," she said. "It's different. When I was young, I did not like to go to school with the teachers looking at your exercises. Then working — this was a difficult time for me. I had to get up at six o'clock and work for eight hours. I'm more free now. I can do what I want when I want. I never think about the things I can't reach. I know my time is limited, so the only thing I have to do is enjoy myself. Like mah-jongg — I will do it to my last day."

Fred's life seemed an unlikely place to look for happiness. He lived alone in a walk-up apartment in Brooklyn's Crown Heights neighborhood that he couldn't clean, separated from the world by thirty-seven stairs it hurt him to climb. By the time I met him he was spending days at a time without leaving the apartment, even though it pained him not to socialize. He had a daughter who was dying of breast cancer and a heart that had already landed him in the hospital a couple of times. His sons owed him money and rarely spoke to him. His brother, the closest person in his life, had lost a leg to diabetes and lived too far for Fred to visit. Yet over the course of the year, when I was feeling low, visits to Fred always chased my demons away.

"How do you define happiness?" he asked me one day. He had gotten news that week that the pastor of his church had died, and he was struck to see that the pastor was much younger than he. We were in his living room amid stacks of old bills and unsorted papers, some left over from hospital stays from years back. He didn't seem to notice the air's stale funk. I said something about happiness being a sense of purpose and worth.

Fred had an easy smile, though he sometimes left his teeth in restaurants. "See, that's not happiness," he said. "Happiness to me is what's happening now. Not the next world; it's not the dance you're going to tonight. If you're not happy at the present time, then you're not happy. Some people say, I get that new fur coat for the winter, or get myself a new automobile, I'll be happy then. But you don't know what's going to happen by that time. Right now are you happy? Like me. I have health problems, but it's been going on a long time, so it's secondary. Sometimes if I say I'm going out tomorrow, and then it rains all day, I'll turn on the TV. I can watch TV, have some ice cream, which I'm not supposed to have, something like that. Yes indeedy."

What I had called happiness was a perspective of my age, at which I was still making my place in the world, looking to the future; Fred described instead a view from old age — taking satisfaction in what was available right now, not hitching it to the future. My definition looked forward; Fred's found fulfillment in the present, because the future might not come.

Fred hadn't always felt this way. When he was younger, he said, he thought happiness was something he had to go out and seize. It led to a lot of mistakes in his life, mostly out of restlessness with what he had. He never married but had six children by four different women, and had maintained close ties with only one daughter. Fred rarely admitted to any regrets, but one afternoon, when we had been talking for a while, he let down his guard. "I played and played and played until I played out," he said. "I wasn't smart enough. I thought I was gonna be healthy, happy, and vigorous and everything else for a hundred years at least. Then I got caught — nobody here to take care of me, and it's all my own fault. I always felt that there was something better out there for me."

Fred had hoped to go to medical school during college, and knew enough about the human body to know that his health problems — diabetes, low blood pressure, an infection in his toes that resisted treatment because his circulation was poor — were serious and not likely to improve much, if at all. But he chose not to dwell on his problems or spend time with people who did. He mostly avoided people his age, especially from his church, because they tended to talk about their physical ailments or those of others. His ailments took enough out of him, he said; why should he give them more of himself willingly? "There used to be a song, I guess it's still out there, 'There's a Brighter Day Somewhere,' " he said. "It goes, 'I'm not going to rest until I find it.' I look at it the same way with illness. This is a short period of time, hopefully, and when I get out and work myself gradually back into physical condition — I got a good outlook on life. It's like the Chesapeake Bay Bridge-Tunnel. The span is too long just to have a bridge, so they had to have a bridge and an underpass. So part of it you're up here, and part of it you're down here, and finally you get to the Eastern Shore. Good days, bad days. But overall it's good days."

Happiness, for Fred, didn't require effort on his part, and came as a kind of peace. All he had to do was sit back and let it wash over him. Life gave him what he needed, if he was wise enough to accept it.

"I had an acquaintance who got one or

two Social Security checks, and now he's gone," Fred said. "And I've been getting twenty-some years of checks, and I'm here. I say thank God. I don't try to examine it or think I'm any better than anyone else, but I just say thank God, and hope that he will continue me on till I'm a hundred and ten. At that time I'll say, okay, I'll make way for other people, and you can just cremate the body instead of taking up a space in the ground that could be some kid's playground. I got a hundred and ten, so I got a while."

Jonas Mekas, too, described happiness as a state of living in the present. Jonas had survived two great disruptions, first when the Soviets invaded his native Lithuania, and then when he was captured by the Nazis and put in a forced labor camp in Germany. After seeing the suffering caused by human drive, he found happiness not in striving for conquest but in relations with other people.

"I'm not happy if I see something or eat something that I like — I'm not happy unless I'm sharing it with others," he said. His most recent feature film, drawn from his life, was called *Out-Takes from the Life of a Happy Man.*

In his Brooklyn loft, in a former shoe factory, he rooted around for a 1974 essay he had written called "On Happiness." Jonas gave himself few material luxuries but hoarded all manner of books, movies, posters, and other artifacts — he slept on a single bed off the kitchen, but paid for his son's college tuition by selling some of his promotional posters for Andy Warhol's 1965 film *My Hustler* for ten thousand dollars apiece. "The junk that I have not thrown out," he said one day, "keeps me alive." He couldn't always find things right away, but he always found them eventually.

The essay was in the form of a letter to the writer Jane Wodening, in which he described some of the deprivations of his youth and how they shaped his views on happiness now. He was most ecstatic, he wrote, stuffing himself with his brother's Lithuanian potato kugelis — burning his tongue, sweating like a madman, "nodding yes to everything." The essay ended with a plate of grapes shared among friends. After all his struggles, he wrote, "This plate is my Paradise. I don't want anything else — no country house, no car, no dacha, no life insurance, no riches. It's this plate of grapes that I want. It's this plate of grapes that makes me really happy. To eat my grapes and enjoy them and want nothing else —

that is happiness, that's what makes me happy."

Hoarding, of course, is a way of remaking the past into the present. Jonas was forever recombining old film footage, publishing old writings. More often we make the future into the present, living vicariously through joys or disasters yet to come. For Jonas, the future was an illusion; he would acknowledge it only when it became the present. "To talk about the future, that's not how my mind works," he said. "Everything's moving into the future, but the future doesn't exist. It's what we create. Our responsibility for the present moment, that's morality. The future of humanity or the family or whatever depends on what you do this moment. If you want the next moment where everything will be better, then you'd better do this moment right."

People often asked him if he was happy, he said, and his response was always the same: of course he was happy. "I don't understand happiness only as someone just always smiling and laughing. It's more like inner happiness, where you feel you have done everything right in your life, you haven't made anybody unhappy. You have a certain kind of peace and balance in yourself, and you are not anxious about what will happen the next minute or the next day. You let it go and you don't worry, and you lead a balanced life. I'm talking about myself."

Social scientists aren't sure why older people aren't more unhappy — and of course, many are, as are people of any age group. Extreme health problems, pain, and poverty hit old people especially hard. Even ordinary physical decline can sap the joy out of life. Yet contrary to stereotypes, most old people aren't sick and frail. They're living independently, in greater numbers and in better health than any cohort before them. At eighty-five and up, only 11 percent live in a nursing home or similar facility, and almost two-thirds say they don't have trouble caring for themselves; elders' poverty rate is well below that of the general population. It's just that the least healthy get the most attention — no one gets a grant to remedy the happiness of old people.

"We study the problems of old age, not the richness," said Monika Ardelt, an associate professor of sociology at the University of Florida, one of the few researchers studying elder wisdom. "At the end of life you have the whole book in front of you. Sometimes younger generations don't want to listen. But you take something away from the last stage of life. Older people still have a lot to offer to us, even if only how to die and age gracefully."

One compelling explanation for the elders' greater contentment comes from the psychologist Laura L. Carstensen, founding director of the Stanford Center on Longevity. Her hypothesis, which she gave the wonky name "socioemotional selectivity," is that older people, knowing they face a limited time in front of them, focus their energies on things that give them pleasure in the moment, whereas young people, with long horizons, seek out new experiences or knowledge that may or may not pay off down the line. Young people fret about the things they don't have and might need later; old people winnow the things they have to the few they most enjoy. Young people kiss frogs hoping they'll turn into princes. Old people kiss their grandchildren. "It's hard to get an eighty-five-year-old to take inorganic chemistry," Carstensen said. Maybe old people live literally like there's no tomorrow.

Now in her early sixties, Carstensen has rounded features and an amused manner that gives her the look of someone laughing at her own jokes. She has spent the last three decades studying the emotional states of older people and how society might adjust to the realities of living longer. Mostly, she said, our culture has yet to grapple with this change. "In our work we see some incredible people, who are doing great things," she told me. "But as a stage of life, there's no guidance."

Carstensen's interest in old people began with a car accident that almost killed her. At twenty-one, with a baby at home and her marriage imploding, she was riding with friends to a Hot Tuna concert when the driver, drunk, rolled their VW minibus over an embankment. Carstensen suffered a broken femur and other fractures, a punctured lung, and temporary blindness from the swelling in her head. Doctors thought she might not survive. She spent the next three weeks in and out of consciousness, and four months in an orthopedics ward with her leg raised in traction, surrounded by three older women who were immobilized with broken hips. She watched the medical staff treat the old women as conditions to be remedied, not autonomous actors in control of their lives. But the old women saw their lives more fully — with ups and downs, and desires that had nothing to do with their injuries. Carstensen was struck by how the medical system encouraged them to give up this sense of self, and give in to passive helplessness. "That was the first lesson I learned about what it's like to be old," she wrote. "We become what our environment encourages us to be."

She enrolled in college and then graduate school, convinced that there was a better way than what she had seen in the orthopedics ward. A big hurdle, she wrote, was to "separate the problems of aging from aging itself. When you are young and impaired, you are expected to fix the problem. When you are old and impaired, you are encouraged to accept it." How much of the helplessness experienced by some old people was a problem of aging, she wondered, and how much was a result of the world telling them what they were supposed to do? How would things be different if instead of thinking of late life as getting old, we thought of it as living long — a gift given to those lucky enough to be born in the right century?

In the early 1990s, she and a team of researchers at Stanford began a decadelong experiment to study the positivity effect. They gave electronic pagers to 184 people between the ages of eighteen and ninety-four and paged them five times a day for a week, asking them to write down immediately how strongly they felt each of nineteen emotions, both positive and negative: happiness, joy, contentment, excitement, pride, accomplishment, interest, amusement, anger, sadness, fear, disgust, guilt, embarrassment, shame, anxiety, irritation, frustration, and boredom. Then they repeated the experiment with the same subjects after five and ten years.

The experiment was not without its awkward moments. One participant, Jan Post, later told an interviewer about being beeped while "doing what husbands and wives are supposed to do." But the results were striking. Older people consistently reported just as many positive emotions as the younger participants, but had fewer negative ones. They also had more mixed emotions, meaning that they didn't let frustration or anxiety keep them from saying they were happy. Consciously or unconsciously, they were making the choice to be happy even when there were reasons to feel otherwise.

Other experiments added nuance to the findings. In one, Carstensen and her colleagues showed participants a series of images and asked them to recall as many as they could. Older people remembered nearly twice as many positive images as negative ones; younger people remembered positive and negative images equally well.

Carstensen's explanation: older people favored the images that pleased them in the moment, while younger people stored all the information away for future use. In another experiment, participants were shown pairs of faces, then a flashing dot where one of the faces had been, and told to press a key when the dot appeared. Old people responded faster when the dot appeared in place of a happy face; young people responded at the same speed for happy or sad faces. This suggested that old people not only remembered pleasing information better, but also registered new pleasing information more fully in the first place. Using functional magnetic resonance imaging, or fMRI, the researchers found that the emotional processing center of older people's brains, the amygdala, fired more actively when they looked at positive images than negative ones; younger brains reacted to both equally. In this, older brains resemble the brains of people who meditate. Psychopaths and people with PTSD, on the other hand, respond to negative stimuli with fireworks in the amygdala.

Each of the elders I spent time with applied this selective memory to their lives. All minimized any hardships of their earlier lives, even if they were struggling with the last chapter. "I've had a good life," John Sorensen said every time we got together. He said he never experienced bias because of his sexuality, even from the kids in high school who called him "Sis" because he didn't play baseball. "I was never teased about it," he said. In sixty years with Walter, he could only remember one argument. Though he recalled other people suffering during the Depression, for him the Wednesday night dinner of rice was his favorite meal of the week.

"I'll never forget coming into the living room once and my dad had a canary on his hand," he said on my second visit. "And my mother was looking at him, and I will never forget the smile on her face. It was like a young girl falling in love. I never saw such a smile on my mother. It was only an instant, because as soon as they saw me it changed. But it was a beautiful memory that's engraved in my mind."

Here was Carstensen's experimental finding replicated in the real world: John remembered the positive emotional experiences but not the negative ones. As with Fred, he constructed reasons to be happy from the resources available to him, notwithstanding the hardships that might have crushed him. He let go of unpleasant memories that would only add to his woes.

If Carstensen was right, it meant that the changes in memory that come with old age have positive as well as negative effects. Instead of foreshadowing other losses to come, that early blank in your memory — the name of an old teacher you can't remember, the ending of a movie you saw just last month — may also be an adaptive compensation for these losses. We forget and we remember because we need to. This means there can be quality of life even with memory loss, a prospect I had never considered. An element of wisdom, then, is learning how to use memory loss as an advantage.

THREE:
WHY OLDER MEANS WISER

"WHEN YOU'RE YOUNG,
YOU HAVE MORE WORRIES."

At first I thought the elders might be holding back because they didn't want to air their grievances in the media. Their generation, unlike mine, is not known for complaining. But as the months went by and the patterns held, I came to realize that their selective memory — vividly recalling the good times and forgetting about the bad — benefited them in their daily lives. If they couldn't control what was happening with their bodies, they could control their past, shaping it toward a positive outcome.

"When I think of my life, I think of it as a happy one," Ruth said, as if past happiness, too, was a choice we can make. The hardships they did remember provided leverage on the present. Didn't they make it through the Great Depression or the slow and grinding death of their spouse?

In our conversations, Ruth often talked about her years spent caring for her dying mother, her dying husband, and an older sister — "the smartest of us" — who died after a long decline from Alzheimer's. These memories seemed not to pain her but to send her to memories of more pleasant times. Her oldest daughter, Judy, who runs an agency serving low-income seniors, said she often saw this resilience in the people she served. "Anybody who makes it to eighty-five or ninety has tremendous strengths," Judy said. "Someone like my mom, she's lost her husband, she's lost her parents; she knows how to deal with loss. Doesn't make it any less painful, but humans are resilient, and we have a lot to learn from older people, who have survived all kinds of things. Aging isn't necessarily pretty, but it doesn't have to be terrible. Money helps. Having family helps. But I've met people who have neither, and are doing fine in old age."

Severe memory loss is a horrible thing, and we rightly fear it, but selective forgetting can be the better part of wisdom. When you're forty-five, it pays to remember all the mistakes you made in your marriage or career, so you can learn from them; at ninety it's better — wiser — to forget, because the memories will only hurt. In midlife you need to know who screwed you on a business deal; in old age you lose nothing by forgetting the grudge. Selective memory also has a reinforcing effect, in which the rich get richer: kids will visit the grandma who tells happy stories from her youth more than the one who stews over past grievances.

One day in Ping Wong's apartment, I asked her what regrets she carried from her ninety years. Ping's apartment was always immaculate, if modest. She had stopped buying clothes for herself, and her sweater was fraying slightly at the neck. She kept up the plants by her window as part of her regular routine. "Very important," she said. "I like the flowers for my health." She shook her head at my question about regrets. "It's impossible," she said. "You can't go back. Let bygones be bygones."

Ping described her daily routine. She liked to sleep late, then heat up breakfast that her home attendant had prepared the night before. The attendant would arrive at ten and do the dishes. Mornings Ping watered the flowers; she used to go to an exercise class in the morning, but she had come to prefer just sitting around. After lunch she took a nap, and at three she went downstairs to play mah-jongg for a couple of hours, always with the same three women from

Guangdong Province in southern China. A good day, she said, was a day when she won. Every evening she talked to her daughter on the phone and went down to the building's activity room to read or talk. She didn't watch TV at night because it hurt her back to sit up, so she sometimes read lying down before bed. A few years back, her daughter had given her a laptop so she could e-mail or Skype with relatives in China, but she had no place for it, and it was too heavy for her to carry around the apartment. She tried a tablet, but her hands were too shaky for a touchscreen.

This left Ping with a small circle of people and activities, made even smaller recently by the death of a close friend from the building. But it was a highly curated circle. Each meant something to her. She didn't spend energy on people she didn't care about or doing things she didn't like. She didn't go to a job she hated or a school where the other students were mean. She didn't worry about getting fired or flunking math. Her biggest concern was that she have enough money for her burial, and she had already secured that. Anxieties about work, marital strains, money worries, time conflicts, day-to-day stress — these were the things that kept me up at night or made me unhappy; for Ping and the other elders, they didn't really exist. Life was easier now, she said. "When you're young, the future is so far away, and you don't know what will happen to you and the world. So when you're young, you have more worries than the elderly. But I don't worry now."

Imagine that: to be free of the future, meaning the sum of all things that probably won't happen, minus the one that will, which is one's death. Even if just for a minute, the feeling is like that of first flight, weightless and free. Most of us live with this future every day, laboring under its weight. To think like an old person is to journey unencumbered.

In the 1980s, a Swedish sociologist named Lars Tornstam was struck by the prevalence of people like Ping, who were contented in old age despite all they had lost. Like me, he discovered that they were easy to find. When he started interviewing them about their lives, they described changes in their values as they got older. One was that they became more selective about how they spent their time and whom they spent it with. Mingling at cocktail parties or chatting up strangers no longer interested them. They weren't looking for new friends or networking for new contacts. Another was that they became less self-concerned, and more aware of being part of a larger whole. Instead of being lonely, they told him they valued having time alone for contemplation. While other social scientists scrambled to develop new ways for old people to keep busy, Tornstam coined the term "gerotranscendence" as a different way to think about old age: not as a period of decline but as a high point, when people transcend material concerns and focus instead on what's really valuable. The years leading up to old age, he reasoned, were preparation for this stage.

In his surveys of people ages 74 to 104, asking how their values had changed since they were 50, nearly three-quarters agreed with the statement "Today I am less interested in superficial social contacts," and two-thirds said, "Today I have more delight in my inner world"; 81 percent agreed with the statement "Today material things mean less." They became more altruistic and more accepting that life included mysteries that they would never solve. This was extraordinary: while they weren't doing the things we think of as growth, like advancing at work or learning new skills, they were still progressing in more profound ways. One of his most striking findings was that older people seemed to live in the past and present simultaneously, blurring the distinction between memories and current experiences. They revisited old conversations, apologized to dead people they had wronged in the past, gave new thanks for old pleasures.

Of course, Tornstam's subjects were Swedes and Danes, who enjoy a famously generous social safety net, but his concept of gerotranscendence has found some currency here. I was introduced to it by Monika Ardelt at the University of Florida, who studies wisdom and aging. Ardelt believes that some of the tendencies found in seniors, like accepting mixed emotions and moderating negative feelings, constitute a kind of wisdom that grows with old age. Wisdom isn't genius or omniscience — it isn't discovering relativity or solving the Middle East crisis — but a competency that comes from experience. Mozart was a genius; your mother is wise. My mother, anyway.

To measure whether older really is wiser, Ardelt created what she called a three-dimensional wisdom scale, or 3D-WS, which plotted wisdom on three axes: cognitive (the ability to understand life); reflective (the ability to look at life from different perspectives); and affective (emotional wisdom). Individuals might be stronger in one dimension, but wise people use all three in ways that cause them to reinforce one another. Using this scale, Ardelt found that for those who start out wise, wisdom does indeed rise with age, and that wisdom corresponds with a greater sense of well-being. The effect was especially pronounced in her studies of people in nursing homes or in hospice, where there is a low sense of well-being. Those who scored higher for wisdom were more content with their lives — as content as people their age living independently. Wisdom leads to better decision-making and more realistic expectations, less disappointment when things don't work out. Old people aren't made stupid by lust for fortunes they can never spend or sexual conquests they can never consummate; they don't froth for vengeance over slights they don't remember.

A shortened time perspective, in young people as well as old, has a way of wiping away petty distractions, Ardelt said. "There's a reduction of ego-centeredness. All the energies that went to shallowness now go to the essence, what's really valuable. Older people in general accept that there's not much time to live and they're okay with it. Not that they're afraid of dy-

68

ing. They're afraid of the dying process. Wise people are more accepting of the dying process."

Jonas Mekas had a simpler explanation for why he was happy. "I think it's normal," he said. Choosing happiness was actually the path of least resistance, much easier than the agitation so many of his friends manufactured for themselves — worrying about things that hadn't happened, striving for things they didn't need, overindulging in drugs, alcohol, or sex. Even his treatment by the Soviets and the Nazis had been good things in the end, he said, because they had led him to New York and the life he created there.

"Yes, I think I have perspective," he said one day in his home. "I know more of what can be changed and what remains the same or can be changed only slightly. Some of my friends think, oh, this can be changed just like that."

Instead of fretting over the things he cannot change, he spent his energies in pursuits that were nourishing to him and others. The choice was his. Why choose things that make him unhappy? "It comes down to what you believe," he said. "I choose art and beauty, vague as those terms are, against ugliness and horrors in which we live today. For somebody to look at a flower or listen to music does something to one, has a positive effect, and being surrounded by ugliness and horror does something negative. So I feel my duty not to betray those poets, scientists, saints, singers, troubadours of the past centuries who did everything that humanity would become more beautiful. I have to continue in my small way their work."

A starting point for wisdom at any age might be to accept that you're going to die — really accept it — and to feel more contented by the limits, not less. Modern medicine encourages us to consider death a test we can win or lose, something presided over by experts in white coats. But the elders offered a wiser perspective. None of us will get out of here alive, so we might as well live while we can. If we died more like our ancestors, I wondered — at home, surrounded by loved ones, the focus of their care — would we live our lives more with an eye toward cultivating that love?

Two thousand years ago, the Stoic philosopher Seneca argued that we should "cherish and love old age; for it is full of pleasure if one knows how to use it. . . . Life is most delightful when it is on the downward slope, but has not yet reached the abrupt decline.

And I myself believe that the period which stands, so to speak, on the edge of the roof, possesses pleasures of its own. Or else the very fact of our not wanting pleasures has taken the place of the pleasures themselves. How comforting it is to have tired out one's appetites, and to have done with them!"

Carstensen quotes the Rabbi Joshua L. Liebman to similar effect: "I often feel that death is not the enemy of life, but its friend, for it is the knowledge that our years are limited which makes them so precious." Old age had forced this knowledge on the elders, some more willingly than others. But surely it is a perspective we don't have to be old to adopt. We just need to choose it. I had six people willing to teach me a happier way to look at life — mine as well as theirs. I had nothing to lose but the stories I already knew.

Four:
Love in the Time of Lipitor
"YOU'RE NEVER TOO OLD FOR SEX."

Helen and Howie were a story that kept surprising. Twenty-one years apart in age, different in temperament, they proclaimed their devotion to each other as if it were the prime accomplishment of their late years. Yet talking to the two of them together was often like holding two conversations at once, one with Helen and one with Howie, surreally disconnected. They didn't complete each other's sentences so much as wait until the other one stopped talking, then shoot off in another direction. Except when they didn't wait.

That winter, I was marking one year together with a woman I'd met through work, my first new relationship since 1980. She was from Kentucky and worked way too hard. It had taken some prodding from the crew at the dog run to get me to ask her to the opera, and even then, neither of us knew whether our first date was a date.

Perhaps I hadn't phrased the question so well. I was living alone in a large apartment that I couldn't afford on my own, still married, trying to figure out what love should be in middle age. So far it was slower to catch fire, certainly, but also less freighted with expectations. We didn't fight, which was new to me. We also didn't need much from each other, so whatever we got was free money. If the elders were a guide, I had another thirty or forty years in front of me; I tried to imagine what I wanted in a companion, or what I had to offer one.

"It's a different kind of love," Helen said one day in her room, beaming at Howie. He was wearing an enameled copper pendant that she had made for him, and she wore a pin that he had made for her. "The second time around is better," she said. "It's closer. Like sometimes Howie doesn't like what I'm watching on television, he goes next door to his room, and when it's over I call him up and say, 'Come on home.' He says, 'I'll be right there.' "

Though they spent most of their waking hours together, and lived only a few feet apart, the telephone played a key role in their relationship. On a July night, when they were watching TV and Helen fell asleep, Howie kissed her on both cheeks and excused himself. "At the door I said, 'Good night, darling, I'll see you tomorrow morning,' " he said. "Then I called her and said, 'I've never loved anyone the way I love the hell out of you.' "

Helen asked Howie to tell me about the car accident he was in after college, which changed the course of his life. "He was in a coma for nine weeks," she said, as if touting her man's accomplishments. Nearly fifty years later, he still formed words very slowly, with gaps between them. He took his time describing the events of that day in 1968. He and some friends were driving south to attend a basketball game in Jackson, Tennessee, when they pulled around a truck and crashed head-on into a car going north. Howie, sitting next to the driver, took the worst of the crash. "Don't ask me where I was thrown," he said. "Take your pick. Did I go through the windshield or the door?" Doctors at the hospital performed an emergency tracheostomy to open his crushed windpipe. Whether the harm to his brain came from the force of the accident or the lack of oxygen he didn't say.

As he told the story, Helen listened sympathetically. Then she offered me a chocolate.

"I was skinny when I came here," she said.

"Now I weigh a hundred forty–something."

Howie seemed to take no notice. He showed off his pendant, a circle with a Star of David cut out of the center. "This was made by the one woman in my life, Helen," he said.

Helen said that Howie could have a chocolate, too. "I'm for men," she said. "I'm not for women." Then she turned to me. "I hope your girlfriend is nice," she said. "Do you have any children? Come again tomorrow."

We had known each other for about half an hour. With Helen — and, as I soon learned, with her daughter — boundaries had little meaning.

Howie went silent for a while; then he said, "I wish we were married but we're not."

Helen wanted me to understand something about Howie. "He doesn't talk much," she said. "Sometimes you can sit by my side for an hour and not say a word. I'll say, Howie, are you there? Never mind. You'll do."

She prompted him, "Tell him you're a college boy. I didn't go. My mother didn't think I was college material."

Helen was a source of fascination to me. After my father's death in 2004, my mother never showed interest in dating other men, and her friends in her senior building were all widows like her. I couldn't imagine my mother in another light. Helen, on the other hand, put great stock in her ability to attract men, especially in a place where women greatly outnumbered men. She dressed with care and wore makeup and jewelry that her daughter gave her; she said she wanted Botox injections.

"Every morning I put lipstick on," Helen said. "I want the people waiting for medications to eat their heart out. I always look nice."

Her daughter, Zoe, fifty-nine, thought she should be more generous. This was a regular theme in their conversations. "But so do other people look nice, don't you think?" she said.

"No, nobody looks nice."

How was it that some people lost interest in companionship in old age, while others made it the center of their lives? After age eighty-five, only 27 percent of Americans are married, and less than 1 percent live with an unmarried partner; 40 percent live alone. In that age group women outnumber men two to one. Ruth and Ping, like my mother, said they had never given much thought to romance after their husbands died. Fred talked about it constantly, even cruising the cashiers at his neighborhood supermarket to see which was the prettiest, but the give-and-take of an actual relationship was not something he wanted at his age — this lion was all growl. Jonas, whose marriage ended in 2004, had a new love as recently as 2007, and made a yearlong video diary in commemoration, inspired by the fourteenth-century humanist Petrarch, who wrote a poem every day for a year to his love, Laura de Noves. But Jonas's relationship had ended, and the diary entries, which he compiled in his "365 Day Project," gave no hint of its nature or denouement. I briefly considered trying to fix John Sorensen up with a man in my mother's building who lost his partner after fifty-nine years, but neither was in shape for a new chapter.

Helen and Howie had somehow taken a step that the others didn't or wouldn't take. It might seem like a simple matter, but it was big and risky: taking on the needs of another person, knowing that those needs would only grow, while their abilities to serve them would only diminish. One partner would survive the other, and probably soon. Helen worried about leaving Howie behind, but the alternative was even harder to consider. In the meantime, being in a relationship meant adapting to each other's habits and idiosyncrasies; it meant compromise. Sometimes I thought they were in love with being in love, and with the status that followed. They were Howie and Helen, *that* couple, and everyone knew it. When Helen announced in May that she wanted to get married — "maybe in summer," she said — it meant another level of risk and commitment.

Or so I thought.

"I'm never too old for anything," she said. "You're never too old for sex."

Meaning she was interested?

"Of course."

Had they done it already?

"No."

Did she want to?

"I guess so. We have to wait till after his hernia operation. You're asking me very personal questions! Tell us about you and your girlfriend." When Helen's daughter, Zoe, weighed in on the marriage question, things only got more complicated.

Helen Auerbach met Bernard Moses on the first day of kindergarten and married him in 1946, after he returned from service in World War II. She was twenty-two. "I never had a chance to have a boyfriend," she said.

"My husband said, 'You're going to marry me,' and we went all through grade school, junior high school, and high school, and then he went into the service, and when he came home we got married." He was a cutter in a menswear factory and smoked Lucky Strikes; she raised three children, "the best mother but a terrible cook," according to her daughter, and went to work first at a dentist's office and then at the Gap after her older son went to college. When her husband died in 2001, she had no interest in dating other men. "I was too busy having a good time," she said. "I didn't think about it. No one was left from my graduation. They were all dead already."

On another visit, when I asked her about dating, she said, "Nobody asked me. I thought, I might as well die."

Howie Zeimer had girlfriends in college but never dated seriously after his car accident. Then things changed in his sixties, when he met a woman named Cher Thompson, "who I thought was the right girl for me," he said. He also thought her name was Tina. She was in her late twenties, freckled, with wide-set brown eyes and a boxer's bump on the bridge of her nose. The two married in 2008. In 2010, when she pleaded guilty to stealing more than $100,000 from

Howie and another man, she told the court, "To John Grant and Mr. Howard Zeimer, I'm sorry I was such an inconvenience." Howie remembered the judge's name, Shlomo Hagler, and said, "He was real nice and considerate to me."

"What are you talking about?" Helen said.

Helen was first to the nursing home. She had a stroke while walking to the store to buy milk, and was found unconscious behind a hospital near her home, her arm badly broken. She was eighty-four, accustomed to walking two hours a day before work, so fast her daughter had trouble keeping up. "I loved to walk," Helen said. "Especially where we lived in Rockland County, the leaves, the trees are so beautiful, and the flowers are all out now. I miss it." She loved her coworkers at the Gap. But after the stroke and the broken arm, suddenly Helen couldn't take care of herself.

"I had to beg her to use a walker," her daughter, Zoe, said. "She wouldn't use it."

Helen didn't want to hear it. "I walk with a cane," she said. "I couldn't walk with one of those ugly walkers, like the silver ones. I couldn't handle it. I looked like a hunchback."

Helen tried staying with her younger son afterward, but the arguments began almost

80

immediately. By the time I met her, the two had not spoken for more than six years. If she and Howie ever got married, she said, she would not invite her son to the wedding. She did not think it was her role to make amends. "Every Mother's Day I think, This year he'll call me. But he didn't."

At the nursing home, she met a man named Paul who made a bracelet in the copper enameling studio and offered it as a gesture of courtship. "He sent it over with a note, 'Meet me in my room at seven-thirty,'" she said. "I said, what the hell is this?"

And?

"And I went," she said. "We used to watch television together. And then some other girl came, he liked her better. But I showed him." Often Helen seemed to be trying out different ways of telling the same story for effect. Another day, speaking of Paul, she said, "I was glad that he found someone that he liked better. He's pretty sick now."

Howie arrived four months after her, in a room near hers. Helen was attractive and on the rebound, dynamic in a way that he wasn't. He was drawn to her immediately, he said. Helen was less impressed.

"I thought nothing of him," she said. Helen tended to speak in extremes, hating things or loving them, sometimes flipping from one to the other in the same conversation. "We were sitting in the television room, and he asked if I could hold his hand and I said, no, I can't do that. I don't know you and you don't know me, and you have a lot of nerve to ask me to do that."

But Howie persisted. "I liked her outgoing, wonderful personality," he said.

"He wouldn't leave me alone," Helen said. "Every time I turned around he was near me."

They had lucked onto a wing of the nursing home where residents were particularly sociable and close. Neighbors visited each other's rooms often, and those who had been there awhile looked after the newcomers. The average stay at the Hebrew Home is only two years, much of it marked by decline, so friendships had to form quickly. Helen thrived in that environment. Her daughter visited regularly and brought food for everyone. Helen shared a room with a generous woman who "used to take care of me like I was one of her children," she said. "She was such a nice lady. When she died I cried so bad."

"I liked it in the beginning," Helen said. "I liked it very much. And then when I met Howie I really liked it."

To Howie, fresh from the death of his mother and his catastrophe with Cher Thompson, Helen seemed vivacious and attentive, despite her spiky exterior. "I thought she could be, and she eventually proved out to be, the love of my life," he said. "I want to be a part of her delightful family, because I basically don't have anybody."

Helen, in turn, noticed that Howie never spoke ill of the other residents, and that he needed someone to care for him. He had a guardian who visited, but no family. Moreover, he liked the Mets; she liked the Mets. He hated the Yankees; she hated the Yankees. In the television room, she let him take her hand.

"From then on we always hold hands," she said. "I thought he was very nice."

The first kiss came shortly after. Helen said she was waiting for it. She wanted him to kiss her. It was delicious, she said.

"You know where we were?" Howie said. He was a demon for details. "We were situated in the living room down the hall."

"They chased us out of there," Helen said. She was always happy to say she had ruffled someone's feathers. "They told us we didn't belong there."

After the first kiss, she said, the next ones "just became automatic. It became part of us. *Delicious.*" Howie was walking on his own in those days, but soon the nursing home staff put him in a wheelchair to reduce the chance of falls. His relationship with Helen continued to develop.

I had wondered, on meeting them, what Helen got out of the relationship, other than his obvious affection. She was more mobile than Howie and faster in conversation. When Howie took too long to finish a sentence, Helen seemed to tune out. And yet their relationship clearly nourished them both. Helen brought the accumulated knowledge from a fifty-seven-year marriage, including thirteen years after her husband's quintuple bypass surgery. Since I was newly separated, and starting on a new relationship, I wondered what she knew about love that I didn't. Her advice to me was practical: "Save your money, because everything is expensive."

She was also certain of what mattered. She had lost the man who had been the center of her life since kindergarten, and later watched friends die at the nursing home, and still found a way to move on. When I asked her what made her life worth living, she said, without hesitation, "I have Howie. I know at night is our time. And I'm glad that he comes in at night. And I watch the clock. They shouldn't have to knock on the door that it's time to go." She said that in six years together they had never had an argument. "You wanna know why?" she said. "Because whatever I say goes. Right, Howie? Yes it does. Wait till I get you home."

Helen thrives on attention and knows how to get it. Often she mentioned how much trouble she was in with the nurses. But from Howie she got something else, someone for whom she could make sacrifices. Since her grandchildren had become adults, she hadn't been needed by anyone the way she was needed by Howie. One day, when she was fretting about the tensions between Zoe and Howie, Helen looked momentarily lost. It was an uncharacteristic mood for her. "So tell us what to do," she said. "I'm looking for directions. What's going to be our life, Howie's and mine? I never accomplished anything in my life. I raised a daughter and two sons; one son don't talk to me. It's going to be seven years already. That's what I accomplished. Sometimes I get like this. I don't know why."

With Howie, she was still useful. The less capable Howie was, the more she could do for him; the more he needed her, the more she got in return. Their asymmetry — all the things that made them an odd match, and made Helen's children resist the relationship — gave direction and purpose to her life. She wasn't sacrificing herself for Howie; she was returning to the role that had given meaning to most of her life. Unlike a younger lover who hopes to change his or her partner, Helen did not expect Howie someday to give her more. She wasn't living in the future, hoping for better things to come. That wasn't the point.

"I take care of him," she said. " 'Cause he's an only child and he had nobody, then when his mother and father died he had no one except me. I tried to be everything to him. I think I am. I'm very motherly to him."

In numerous studies, researchers have found that seniors who feel useful to others live longer and better, with fewer disabilities, greater mobility, and more resilience to arthritis pain. Helen did not know about this research. What she knew was laundry. "I do his clothes," she said one day. "I take them down to the washing machine. Don't tell my daughter. Then I'll get killed. I don't feel like getting killed yet. I still got three more years."

For much of her life, this was the role that validated her. She loved cleaning — not cooking, but cleaning — and taking care of her three children, following in the footsteps of her own mother. "My mother was such a good woman," she said. "Whoever we brought home she always had enough to give them dinner. 'Sit down, you'll eat.' She wasn't wild about my husband, but she tolerated him. She was my best friend. She worked so hard. I watched her grow old. I loved her." Zoe said Helen was the same way — loved her friends, hated her boyfriends. "She was invited to all the kids' parties," Zoe said.

Several times in our conversations during the year, Helen cried when she talked about her mother, who died in 1969. "I still dream about her," Helen said. Her parents had both moved from Russia to a sparsely developed tract just north of New York City early in the last century, with an icebox and a coal stove to heat the house. Her father worked in the garment industry; her mother raised Helen and her three sisters, all blonde and pretty. "If you saw one of us, you saw all of us," Helen said. When her mother had a stroke, Helen and her sisters took care of her. "I used to sleep with her many a night," Helen said. " 'Cause I loved her so much. That was the hardest period. And I was always afraid of her dying.

"When I lost my mother I was lost," she

said. "I lost everything."

For Helen, getting older had meant first watching her mother die, then losing her own role as a mother. Now her daughter was the one taking care of her. "Sorry, Ma, but it's like having a kid back in school again," Zoe said one day after Helen had fallen in her room. "I'm going through what I did for my daughter, and what you did for me. It's definitely a whole new ball game."

Helen's fall had shown her how far the roles had changed. It was six o'clock in the morning, and she had been on her way to get her medications — up early, she said, "because I don't want to miss anything." Suddenly she was on the floor and couldn't get up. "I was banging and banging and nobody heard me. I slid on my behind all the way to the door and I opened the door and I said, 'Please somebody help me.' And they brought a wheelchair and put me in a wheelchair, and they sent me where you go to get help. I went to rehab every day. They only gave me a week. Zoe gave it to them. So they gave me two more weeks."

Helen's new role in this mother-daughter relationship had its benefits, but it was not the one by which she had measured herself for so long. Wasn't she still the mother? Now she was answering to Zoe, as her children had once answered to her. "She takes charge of me," Helen said. "She calls up, 'Did you do exercises today?' Sometimes I lie. I don't like lying but I have to sometimes. She never got the chance to do that before I came here. When she comes she says, 'Gee, Mom, you got a fat stomach.' She doesn't spare the rod." When I pointed out that Zoe said these things out of love, Helen was not assuaged. "I always say, 'Don't love me so much,' " she said. " 'I'm not going to be here forever.' She says, 'Where are you going?' "

It was a long train ride to see Helen, and I often thought about my own marriage on the ride back. Much of our energy in the marriage had been focused on raising our son, and once he was grown, we had nothing to replace it. We needed a new way to be together — new roles and new supports — but we were too worn down or too ossified to find them. I was at the kitchen sink when my wife casually suggested we get divorced. I don't think I even interrupted my dishwashing. We were a car that had run out of gas, banged up by so many miles on the road. Walking away was an easy decision. I felt fatigue more than loss; the loss, I realized, had come years ago.

The British cultural critic Terry Eagleton

writes that the meaning of life lies in learning how to form mutually enriching relationships, like musicians in a jazz ensemble, who create melodic openings for the other players by inventing melody lines for themselves. Love, he writes, "means creating for another the space in which he might flourish, at the same time as he does this for you. The fulfilment of each becomes the ground for the fulfilment of the other. When we realize our natures in this way, we are at our best." This is perhaps a more aspirational spin on the Buddhist idea that love is wishing for the happiness of the beloved. I ran Eagleton's formula by my wife once, after we split up, saying that our marriage had died when we stopped trying to help each other be our best. She said no, the problem was that I was an asshole. She was usually right about things. She also believed in zero-sum equations. But Howie, for all his disabilities, did this for Helen, and she did the same for him. Together they were more than the sum of their parts.

If my year with the elders was also to be a love story, this was a lesson that I needed to learn: that in a relationship, sometimes taking — allowing the other person to do something for you, rather than insisting on doing it yourself — is also a kind of giving.

The same applies in friendships or business relationships. True generosity includes enabling others to be generous. Howie didn't have much choice, because he genuinely needed the care that Helen gave him, but there was still something to be learned from the way both accepted the arrangement, he as much as she. In a place where there were attendants on hand to do anything for her, Howie gave her space to do things for him.

Old age at some point forces us to accept help from other people. It can be hard on the ego, perhaps, because it means acknowledging that we are not in control of the world. But it also gives something valuable to the people who help us. For Helen and Howie it freed them from the destructive math that poisons relationships — the constant questioning of whether you're giving too much or getting too little in return. Of course they were giving too much. They wouldn't want it any other way.

Over the course of the year, their plans for marriage came and went and came and went, with Zoe always the blocking character. It was a dance among three people who needed one another. All knew the nursing home was the last stop for Helen and Howie. What they wanted was the best life

91

possible in the time they had left. They had already outlasted most of the people they met when they moved in. Whenever I left I thought I'd be back, but I couldn't be sure.

"I never thought about being old," Helen said one day. "But it is old. Ninety is old. Your life goes so quick. I remember when I was thirteen. I used to come home for lunch every day. And I was going down the hill and I said, 'Hey, I'm thirteen years old already.' And here I am, ninety. It's all right.

"When I was fifty years old, it was the worst day in my life," she said. " 'Cause I was getting old. But now it's not so bad. 'Cause I met Howie." She mimed kisses in Howie's direction. "And nobody tells me what to do."

The train back from Riverdale ran south along the eastern shore of the Hudson River, with the afternoon sun slanting through the windows or, if it was really late, glistening off the rippled water. I'd begin the trip replaying my conversations of the hours before, now with the benefit of a little distance. At ninety, living in a nursing home, Helen had made a life for herself that was fuller and more purposeful than those of people I knew who were half her age. She was essential to the two people she cared most about. Would she and Howie ever get married? Would they have sex? These questions made for great narrative tension, but seemed less important in her life. Loving Howie and Zoe, and being loved by them, meant loving the life she had and the body she was in, as they were right this minute.

This seemed as good a definition of happiness as any I've come across. Helen found someone who needed her; she met his needs and she accepted his love in return. They responded not to each other's perfections but to each other's gaps. Each flourished by giving the other what he or she needed — that is, by enabling the other to flourish. It wasn't an easy formula, but it was one that I could strive for in my own relationships. Happiness wasn't something esoteric but an appreciation of the things already available in our lives. Sometimes it was an old woman in a nursing home with a partner in a wheelchair, telling the same story for the nineteenth time.

How to be happy? Here was a start. Accept whatever kindnesses people offer you, and repay with what you can. Let a friend buy you lunch, then do her a solid in return. You'll benefit from the favors you receive, but even more from the ones you perform. Don't begrudge the people who need you; thank them for letting you help them. Give up the obsession with self-reliance; it's a myth, anyway. None of these comes naturally to me, and even as I write them now, they seem too pat. But in Helen and Howie I saw them in action, again and again, and here is what I saw: they worked. They weren't genius; they were wisdom.

The trains were usually uncrowded during my trip home, a buffer zone between the nursing home and the crush of Grand Central Terminal, and the rocking motion wrapped the afternoon in a soft cocoon. The day was over and whatever wasn't done would remain undone. If there was no one nearby I'd call my girlfriend to check in, and if it was a good day I'd remember to tell her that I loved her. After visiting Helen and Howie, seeing the odd ways that they sustained each other, it was almost always a good day.

FIVE:
ON THE OTHER HAND . . .

"HOW ELSE CAN I PUT IT?
I WASN'T INTERESTED."

It was tempting to think, looking at Howie and Helen, that they had found what everyone their age wanted: a second (or third, or ninth) chance at love, a new beginning, a companion to share their days and nights. Romantic love, sex, camaraderie, laundry — these bring out the most in us, whatever our age. Without them, the data suggest a dour tale. People who live alone have more health problems and higher rates of depression and die earlier, and the risks of social isolation increase with age. In the past, old people who outlived their spouses could count on their children or other relatives for companionship, but these days only one in five people ages eighty-five and up lives with family members. As I climbed the stairs to Fred Jones's solitary apartment, or rode the long subway trip out to Ruth Willig's, I expected to see the effects of this isolation, which gerontologists compare to those of smoking.

But once again, the elders surprised me. Though they complained about other things missing from their lives, none said he or she wanted a mate.

"Oh no," Fred said when I asked him about the prospect of pairing up. "I'm just going to take it easy." It was a few days after his eighty-eighth birthday, and he'd boasted about two women fighting over which one would get to celebrate the day with him. In the end neither had come through, and he'd spent it alone, but he didn't seem disappointed. As he'd gotten older, he said, the solitary life suited him. His hours were his own, and he didn't have to accommodate anyone else's habits or tastes. If he felt like staying up all night or spending the day in his pajamas, there was no one around to tell him he couldn't. After his last live-in girlfriend, in 1979, he'd vowed to wait five years before finding another, then extended it to ten. Then, as more time passed, he found that he liked having the apartment to himself.

"I never wanted to settle down," he said. "I always felt that there was something better out there for me. I said, after fifty. But fifty came so fast, I said, after sixty I was going to get married and settle down. And then sixty and seventy came so fast, I didn't do it. Now I see a girl once in a while, she has a car. I'm not walking so good. I told her, look, all you're going to get out of me is my favorite dishes, Chinese food. It's no sexual thing, not even romantic kissing. I give her a little smack on the cheek, that's about it."

Fred, I thought, could use a mate: someone to share meals and expenses, give him reasons to turn on the charm. He was a flatterer who liked being flattered, and often reminded me that he was known as a sharp dresser, a "bon vivant." Though he was always cheery during my visits, I wondered what he was like during the long stretches when no one stopped by. If he had a partner they could go to church or on walks together, and rediscover the joys of sex, whatever these meant at his age. It would also force him into a more regular schedule, which might stabilize his diet and help him remember to take his medications — all buffers against the diabetes that was behind the ulcerous infections in his toes. Maybe a partner would even come with an apartment in an elevator building.

Fred would have none of it. "My brother got mad at me, said 'Are you crazy?' " he said. " 'If she looks good and you think she's got a home, talk to her.' I haven't done it. Now I don't feel like doing it. If she says, 'Honey, go out there and clean the car,' if I feel good, okay. If I don't, I probably won't do it, and she'll probably get upset." Besides, he said, "Most of them are too old for me."

Fred was a complicated case, because he often asked me to fix him up with "one of those fine chicks" he thought I knew. "Maybe I can persuade some lady to come over here and live with me and let me slap on her butt once in a while," he said. He could sense the clutter in his apartment closing in on him, especially since his daughter had become too sick to visit regularly. But sex, which had been the driving force for so much of his life, had lost its hold over him, and he over it — a common side effect of chronic diabetes. "I didn't think I'd ever turn against sex," he said, "but after maybe about my seventy-eighth birthday, I had several opportunities, and I just played around with the breasts, but that was about it. I just didn't feel like it. At least I don't have to worry about getting in any trouble now." When I asked him what he looked forward to in his eighty-ninth year, sex was a part of it, but an oblique part.

"Try to eat my three meals a day, talk to

the ladies," he said. "Visit them, maybe they visit me, go to church, and in summertime stand in front of the door downstairs, watch the women getting off work. I just want to live and keep happy, hope my brother continues on in a good life. I want to start visiting him more often." In the time I spent with Fred, he was able to do none of these things.

A particularly damaging myth about old age is that people no longer work or have sex — just about the two most belittling things you can say about someone in America. But neither of these is necessarily true. Love among the elderly is a topic that makes many people squeamish, especially when it involves sex — and doubly if the elderly happen to be your parents, which they probably are. Sagging skin, fragile bones, poor circulation, growing memory gaps — these aren't exactly the stuff celebrated in Victoria's Secret ads or chick flicks. People in my mother's generation rarely watched their own parents remarry or date in old age, and many reached their eighties and nineties with limited romantic experience. They'd married young and stayed married. In a University of Chicago study called the National Social Life, Health, and Aging

Project, only one in five women ages seventy-five to eighty-five said they had had more than two sexual partners in their lifetime, and only half of men. If new love was going to have a place for their age group now, they were going to have to invent it, without role models or guidance.

Sociologists expect big changes to come with the baby boomers, who already wrought one sexual revolution. But some elders have always enjoyed robust sex lives. A 2010 study by researchers at Indiana University's Center for Sexual Health Promotion reported that 20 to 30 percent of men and women were still sexually active well into their eighties. (Men ages seventy and up, notably, were giving oral sex more often than receiving it, and women weren't doing much of either, most likely because they had outlived their mates.)

But with age, sex can entail new complications. After age eighty-five, more than one-quarter of people say they have some cognitive difficulty. Sex with dementia raises questions of consent that we are only beginning to grapple with, even as more people live long enough to enter that territory. Many nursing homes, where people with dementia tend to land, have been slow to draft formal policies for their staffs on how to deal with residents who want to have sex, let alone communicating guidelines to residents and their families. So sex becomes like death: people do it but nobody talks about it, at least not in public.

The facility where Helen and Howie live, the Hebrew Home at Riverdale, is an exception to this rule, as in many things. Since the 1990s the home has had a policy to foster intimate relationships for residents, including those with Alzheimer's, and to permit sexually explicit literature or videos. Nurses watch for changes in behavior that might signal one person is unhappy in a relationship, like a loss of appetite (the staff also holds monthly services to acknowledge residents' deaths, which is even rarer among facilities). Recently the home added a dating service, called G-Date, or Grandparent Date, but it has not been a smash: at a recent count, only about 40 of the facility's 870 residents were in relationships. Many had nursed their spouses through long, emotionally draining deaths, and did not want to do so again.

Ruth Willig knew this experience well. By the time I started visiting her, her husband had been dead for twenty-one years, and in that time she had never dated. When I asked her what she'd had to give up in old age, she paused and said, "Of course the obvious one is sex, but that didn't bother me that much. And I used to love to walk." She made it clear that she missed the latter more.

Gerontologists often worry about people like Ruth, who live alone and choose not to participate in group activities, including those they once enjoyed. "Social isolation kills," said Donna M. Corrado, commissioner of New York's Department for the Aging. "People don't get out, don't eat, don't take their medication, die early." Often when I visited Ruth, she mentioned a recent outing or exercise class that she'd considered but decided against. A happy social life, for her, was the one she had lost when she left her old building.

Yet it is also possible that people simply lose interest in certain kinds of social contact as they get older, instead applying their energies to people and relationships they find more meaningful. Ruth sometimes worried about her children or grandchildren, but she never mentioned being lonely. Sociologists see this as a kind of curation: with limited time in front of them, older people try to fill it with people who sustain them, and they let go of those who tire them out or make demands. Instead of making new connections, they rely more heavily on the ones they have. Finding a mate isn't as important as keeping strong social ties, and these are only valuable if they are positive in nature; being in a bad relationship or spending time with toxic relatives is no better for elders than for young people. As Laura Carstensen writes, "Bad relationships may be more harmful than good relationships are beneficial."

Ruth grew up in the Brownsville neighborhood in Brooklyn, once called the Jerusalem of America, with more than seventy synagogues and residents who included Mel Brooks, Danny Kaye, Norman Podhoretz, and Jerry Stiller. Her street was unpaved, and a woman on the block kept a goat. Like Helen, she met her husband in childhood and never saw a need to date other boys. She was eleven and he was a friend from the neighborhood, from a poor family that refused to go on relief during the Depression. They were together until the war separated them.

Unlike Helen, Ruth always planned for an advanced education and a career. She was the youngest of four children, the rebel of the family. At sixteen, with her male classmates off to war, Ruth went to Brooklyn College, which was free at the time, and studied bacteriology. She exchanged letters with her future husband during the war, and when he came home they married and moved by the beach in Far Rockaway. They were part of the postwar boom, raising two sons and two daughters.

When I met her at ninety-one, Ruth was losing some mobility because of arterial blockage in one leg, but was still intellectually curious, in sporadic contact with the friends she'd made since her husband's death and in daily contact with her children. "Every morning I have to send an e-mail to all my four children," she said. "If I don't, I'll get a call, 'Mom, are you okay?' I tell them, what are you worried about, I'm in a place like this, I'm supposed to be watched." If her Internet access goes down, she knows by now to call her daughter before the kids start to panic.

Ruth was determined not to go gentle into old age. She wore her white hair cut short and ironed her clothes before leaving her apartment, but she dressed more for function than for flair. A well-pressed blouse was like a clean home — it was something she could control, a refusal to quit. She took eight medications, including an anti-depressant for occasional dizzy spells, but overall her health was good. She'd discovered she could get library books delivered to her without going to a branch. Each time I visited she was reading something new — it was what she did instead of socializing or going on the building's trips.

"Do I want to live to a hundred?" she asked one day. "Not especially. I was happy to make ninety, I have to tell you that. I wonder what I'll die from. All of us at our age, my age, we say we want to die fast. We think of our children. We don't want to — 'burden' them is the old word. But also, you don't want to suffer that much. I think, 'Is it going to be cancer? Is it going to be my heart again? Will I just drop dead?' That's what I do think about. I don't brood about it."

She didn't think about getting old, she said, "because that would really make me depressed."

Ruth, more than the others, was someone with whom I could talk about my mother. Both were educated career women who lived in New York City but weren't quite of it, and who had raised their families outside the central metropolis. Ruth was from a bygone Brooklyn that didn't exist anymore, and my mother was from Pennsylvania Dutch country, and had raised her three sons in New Jersey. Both had poured a lot of themselves into their roles as wives, then mothers, and now didn't know where to find roles that made them feel useful. Neither had dated after their husbands died.

These days, Ruth said, she missed being needed. Her children were all grown, and her grandchildren needed little from her. "What's the good of living anymore, at this point — for me?" she said one day. I learned over time that she was always in darker spirits in the winter, when the days were short and the climate inhospitable. The season made her feel her age. Other than e-mailing her children to say she was still alive, she didn't have any responsibilities now, she said. "Maybe that's what I'm missing," she said. "I really am not needed by anyone, come to think of it. I'm certainly cared for. I know there's a lot of love from them, and I feel it. But outside of providing money for them when I can, I don't have any . . . I guess that's a problem of living older."

Yet she made it clear that she did not want to share her life with a man again. Her life with her husband had been organized around family and work, and they had sent all four children to college. When her husband developed stage IV lymphoma in his early fifties, Ruth nursed him through harsh chemotherapy and an opportunistic case of shingles that blistered his skin. But the treatments knocked the cancer into remission, allowing him another ten years of good health. It was time they hadn't expected. When he developed pancreatic cancer in 1994, this time the illness took a toll on her as well — she had a heart attack in his room at Sloan Kettering Memorial Hospital. He was gone before the year's end.

After that, she said, "I just never thought of caring for anybody else. It never occurred to me."

Occasionally during the year I asked Ruth about the years she'd spent caring for sick loved ones — not just her husband, but also her mother and an older sister who had Alzheimer's. Ruth made little of her sacrifices, saying, "When you do it out of love you don't really think anything of it. Judy says, 'Ma, you don't remember.' I guess I was a caregiver. But I never begrudged."

Marriage, for Ruth, had provided decades of companionship and four children. She and her husband had grown up together and gotten old together; when she heard stories about women her age finding new partners, the rewards seemed trivial by comparison, and the compromises too great. To start a new relationship, with all the responsibilities it entailed, would be a leap into the unknown, and there was enough uncertainty in her life. Shortly after her husband died, a friend from their temple lost his wife. The two couples had socialized together and had interests in common. When he called and asked her to lunch, she could tell that he was lonely and needed someone. She, on the other hand, didn't. She was busy remaking her life, still driving a car, meeting new friends at a community center near her home. "I went to lunch with him, but I couldn't do it," she said. "I really was very unhappy with it. And I kept seeing him afterwards, and he really needed somebody, so finally I said, 'Look, it's not you,' which it wasn't. I just was not interested in other men. I never had another chance, but I never cared. I loved my husband and we had a wonderful marriage. I didn't feel the need to have another man in my life. How else can I put it? I wasn't interested."

She added, "Some women, on the other hand, really want to have somebody."

Ruth's story is not uncommon. Couples who get old together tend to say their marriages improve with age. They're more tolerant of small disagreements, slower to fight, more ready to forgive afterward. But starting a new relationship, especially after the death of a long-term companion, is a lot of work. More often, elders say they want a network of connections — someone to eat breakfast with, someone to talk with about current events, et cetera. Those who build these networks throughout their lives are in better position in old age, but it is also possible to start them later.

One night in my mother's apartment, I asked her why she'd never dated after my father died. It was almost twelve years since his death, and in that time she had lost the capacity to walk more than a few steps without a walker or wheelchair, but she was still as sharp as ever. Once she had asked me to buy her marijuana to relieve her back pain, thinking an illegal drug must be more powerful than the superstrength opioids she was taking, but the smoke irritated her lungs, so the weed — which she'd hidden from her aide — remained unsmoked, probably does to this day. We talked about my father and his last days, which she remembered differently than I did.

The last time I saw him in good shape was in the fall of 2004, at a book party near my home in the East Village. He drove in from New Jersey with my mother — he'd given up long drives after falling asleep behind the wheel on a trip to North Carolina, but still drove short distances — and was glowing to be among my friends and colleagues. Back home, though, he was starting to become agitated at night, sleepwalking, talking nonsense to my mother. He had had two heart attacks and at least one minor stroke, and took so many overlapping medications that any changes in his behavior might have been written off as pharmaceutical in nature. "I thought he was just eccentric," my mother said. But as he wandered the house, my mother felt herself alone with a responsibility she might not be able to manage. Around Halloween he collapsed in the middle of the night and couldn't explain where he'd been going.

When my mother thought about dating other men, she thought about the six or seven weeks that had followed. My father moved from the hospital to a nursing home for rehab, then home for a few days, then to a second hospital, where there was little hope that he would ever leave. His kidneys, heart, and lungs were all spiraling downward, each accelerating the others' decline. Cascade iatrogenesis, it's called, meaning your dominoes are cooked. He wasn't getting enough oxygen to his brain, and he was

110

often adrift, reliving conversations from his Alabama childhood — a pleasant alternative to the dismal surround of his hospital room. One day he told me that the world was becoming a better place, and that the evidence he had for this was his three sons. That was always his attitude toward life, but he never would have expressed it so personally. I would like to say that those were the last words he said to me, but I also remember him saying quite clearly, after I had tried to replace an oxygen mask on his face, "I'm going to die," meaning "Why are you putting me through this?"

His trials were not over yet. After some family discussion, we authorized the doctors to insert a ventilator tube down his throat to pump oxygen-rich air into his lungs. This meant he couldn't talk or put food or water in his mouth. He was now immobile, eyes staring upward, hands tied at his sides to keep him from yanking out the tube. We said our goodbyes, each in his or her own way. It didn't last long, maybe a day or two, before we told the doctors to remove the tube. But the memory of those last days, and the guilt of having approved the ventilator, never left my mother.

It was the first thing she mentioned when I asked her about dating. "I wouldn't want to do that again," she said. "You don't know what it was like when your father died. He was in terrible shape. And he suffered so. In fact, when he went into the hospital the last time, before he went in he told me he wanted to die. And I regret that I let them continue trying to revive him. But you boys came in and you said, 'We want to give Dad every chance.' And I didn't have the strength to say no." After that experience, she said, "I just could never go through that with another person. It was horrible to watch."

My parents were both from close-knit communities where most people tended to stay, and they met in Greenwich Village, where everyone was from somewhere else. They were children of the 1930s, raised by parents who were children of the 1910s. They stressed independence, hard work, frugality, not calling attention to yourself, "fulfilling your potentialities," as my father said in almost any long conversation. My mother was an only child, the first in her Pennsylvania family to go to college. My father left Alabama for the war and never went back. Both were better at severing ties than making them. These traits they passed on to their children. I don't remember ever seeing them hugging or kissing.

"I've always been pretty independent in

mind," my mother told me. "Willful, I guess. Foolhardy. I always felt in the marriage that I was never completely immersed in that, though at the time I had the children I didn't have much freedom to do anything. I always felt I liked to be independent and I was happier when I had a job." When I asked if she considered it a happy marriage, she said, "I never thought about it. There are always times in any marriage where you feel like walking out. But we had too much together, too many years. Everybody who has been married a long time feels like walking out at one time or another. But first of all, marriage is a vow that you take and you don't break it. Certainly not easily."

Where Ruth focused on the good times in her marriage, feeling any new relationship could not measure up, my mother focused on the sadness of my father's last days, an experience she never wanted to relive. But the results were the same.

One day my mother surprised me by talking about a man who had taken an interest in her. It was in the first couple of years after she moved into the building, maybe a decade in the past, and she made a point to say that it was really nothing. His name was Frank and he was Irish, and when he moved into the building his clothes were falling off his skeletal frame. "He came in and he looked terrible, so I thought nobody else would want him," she said. Some women in the building tended to flock around any decent-looking new men, but Frank didn't draw that kind of attention, she said.

"He had lost a lot of weight. I guess he had been very sick. So I started having breakfast with him, and I found him very interesting. He was an economist, and I had studied economics in school. He was going to start a blog and he was going to show me how to do that. I was not in love with him. He was just a nice person to talk to, especially as a relief from the women that I always sat with. It was just a whim. It wasn't an event. I wasn't in love with him."

Frank, it turned out, was not long for the building. After a few weeks of breakfasts, one day he wasn't there — a typical occurrence in buildings like hers, where privacy laws and perhaps a fear of upsetting the other residents prevent the staff from acknowledging a sudden absence. It was only through the informal grapevine that she learned that Frank had died. If he had family, she never knew about them.

"That was my one adventure," she said. "But I really just wanted to make a friend with him."

It is a received wisdom in our time that married people live longer. The logic is compelling: Partners help each other keep medical appointments, follow low-sodium diets, call 911 if one falls; together, they're less likely to be poor. Companionship is also good for the spirit, especially when our social networks start shrinking. But when the psychologists Howard S. Friedman and Leslie R. Martin drilled deeper into the data on marriage and longevity, they found that the story was more nuanced. What was true was that married *men* lived longer. Unmarried women, they found, live as long as their married counterparts, often with more leisure time to devote to themselves. In a study that followed 1,500 Californians for eight decades, Friedman and Martin found that "widowed women tended to thrive — they lived longer than the still-married women." They built social networks, herded their kids, did all the things they put off when their husbands were ill. Widowed men, on the other hand, tended to go quickly.

It seemed to me that my mother's life, rather than constricting after my father's death, was also opening up. She had regular friends for the first time that I knew of, and nobody to look after but herself. She took up Spanish, joined a ceramics class, and went to concerts with her female friends, who expected nothing of her but her company. She was lonely, I think, but not just lonely. With Frank the economist, she had the romance of romance — not a man in her life but the possibility of a man, without any obligations on her part. It didn't matter that she wasn't in love with him. The last thing she needed was another person to take care of.

Ruth, Helen, Ping, and John had all similarly nursed their partners through their deaths, a generational rite shared mainly by women. John's friends especially worried about how he would go on after Walter — how he would remain socially active, pay his bills, take his medications, navigate the city with his failing eyesight. During the AIDS crisis, many gay men nursed their partners through horrific deaths, but older gay men being widowed after decades together — usually without children, for obvious reasons — is something new.

Yet John, like Ruth and my mother, had no interest in other men after Walter died. He still thought about sex all the time, and had something of a crush on Hugh Grant, but the sex was all in his head now, he said. "Interest, yes. Capabilities, none. I have a sexual urge all the time, but there's nothing to be done about it. It doesn't work anymore. And I guess I dream about sex. I sure did love it." Anatomically, he said, he was reverting to boyhood.

John Sorensen first saw Walter Caron at a party in the summer of 1950, when Walter was visiting New York from Boston. John had his eye on two other men that night, but they turned out to be interested in each other. "No luck," he said. "So I thought, I'll try Walter." Walter had the dark good looks of the actor Josh Brolin; John was taller and fair, ambitious in his career as a decorator. Though Walter was a couple of years older, he was very limited in his romantic experience. Friends warned him that John was too fast for him. They went home to John's apartment on Washington Square, expecting little more than a night together.

"I never expected to have a lasting affair," John said. "I didn't think it happened between two men. And it did. I'd been going with him for three weeks, and I still didn't think it was a long-term thing. And then he was away and one of my usual tricks came by, and I turned him down. 'Oh, wait, what's going on here, that I turned a trick down?' It wasn't until a month or two later that I admitted to myself that I'd fallen in love with him. That was one of the best decisions I ever made." The following Christmas Eve — two days before John's twenty-ninth birthday — they moved in together, and stayed together until Walter's death in 2009.

Since my own marriage had just ended, I asked all the elders the secret to a long relationship. Their answers, invariably, seemed too simple. "If you're going to be together, you better have an awful lot in common," John said. "And you have to learn that you don't always agree. We did most of the time. But you don't make it an issue. If you don't agree on something, you don't agree. I was brought up in a household where my father was a dyed-in-the-wool Democrat, and my mother was basically a Republican."

This struck me as too little to learn from sixty years together. Everyone knows that they should try to get along. But over the year, the wisdom in John's remark gradually sunk in. I thought about the times I'd gotten angry that my wife could be so repeatedly wrong about something, despite my efforts to correct her. How could she want to go to Cape Cod on vacation, when she didn't swim and didn't like the sun? And what about those times she didn't want to have sex, just because she was freaking out about work? We argued about the same things year after year, even month after month, rather than just accepting the other's views as valid. Instead we each expected the other to change, and got mad when it didn't happen.

John's insight, then, was not so simple. There's nothing easy about accepting things that you don't believe. John, for example, was rigid in his opinions about how a home should look or a tenor should sing an aria. These judgments were who he was. But with Walter, he was willing not just to be swayed by Walter's opinions, but to embrace them even if he wasn't, just because they were Walter's. I knew successful people who thought they were open-minded because they were willing to listen to opposing views before rejecting them. But wisdom, John was saying, lay in accepting them even when you listened and weren't persuaded.

In the time I spent with John, it never saddened him to talk about Walter, even to talk about Walter's death. John often had trouble with short-term memory, but memories of Walter came readily and in living color. I'm not sure how many John actually had — he tended to repeat the same few over and over, sometimes in the same words. My transcripts from interviews in the beginning of the year were largely interchangeable with ones from the end. The past had a hold on John, and its grip was a loving embrace.

"Grieving?" he said one day. "I'm still grieving. I miss him terribly. Sometimes I'll turn over and he's not there and I'll wake up. Once in a while it's almost like he's here. One time I was watching television and I started to talk to him about the show, and then I realized he wasn't there. Other times I forget that he's not here. He's a wonderful guy."

For John, Walter was a constant presence, even though that presence was all about absence. It's possible that he thought about Walter more in death than he did when Walter was alive and didn't need to be conjured. In life, Walter was an old man — or a middle-aged man or a young man. In death, he was all those things at once, as vivid as John's capacity to remember him. He was a story over which John had control, from which John could edit out whatever didn't fit the narrative. In life one's partner is often boring or mundane, but in memory he never is.

John's loss was different from my mother's or Ruth's, because it still felt like yesterday to him. He'd never tried to rebuild his life. He'd never wanted to: rebuilding would increase the distance between him and Walter. Instead, he embedded bits of Walter throughout their apartment, so that Walter was never really gone. The uncomfortable Louis XVI chairs, their silk damask now threadbare, were memories of when John sat in them with Walter; the sofa, now misshapen, was a lumpy memory of the day Walter found it in a Goodwill shop and called John from the nearest pay phone, knowing he could make it beautiful. And if Walter was still young and handsome in these memories, so was John. As long as John didn't change the apartment, the life it held was still available to him.

One thing he had learned in his nine decades was how to comfort himself. "They give me a pill for depression," he said. "But I'm always in a good mood. I feel sorry for myself once in a while, and I get angry. But if I'm listening to music I'm reasonably content. Not what I want to be, but as much as I'm ever going to have." He recalled recently listening to the radio and hearing Tchaikovsky's Fifth Symphony, which he knew very well but hadn't heard in twenty

121

years. As he closed his eyes at the memory, the stress lines at his temples seemed to release the day's frustrations. "I was just smiling," he said. "I'd forgotten it and yet I remembered every bit of it. It was wonderful to hear it again. Music can really get me going sometimes."

John's conversational steps were familiar to me after a while. Remembering Walter would make him think of music, and music would set loose all sorts of memories. In this way, Walter was still the center of his life, an active force. Where John's eyes were failing, Walter opened a world of visual sensations. One day in his living room, during a long discussion of their social life together, John described a Monday night at the Metropolitan Opera House, when the women from New York's high society came out in their finest jewels and gowns, and the men wore white ties and tails. He especially admired the way one woman dealt with her frailty and old age. "There was a lady called George Washington Kavanaugh, she had a tiara on, bracelets up to here," he said. "Just before the lights went down, she would arrive with two men who would hold her. She had a cane. She'd give them the cane, stand up straight, and walk down the aisle alone while the lights were going down. She was old. And she could hardly walk."

It occurred to me that John was still making that walk for Walter — refusing a wheelchair or walker in the way that Lady Kavanaugh left the support of her minders, timing her entrance so she was the last sight people saw before the lights went down. At ninety-one, John knew he didn't have too many steps to navigate on his own, and he was going to walk them in a style that would honor his relationship with Walter. In his memories Walter was always at his best, which meant John was at his best, too. Love gave him a connection to what he'd lost, even if it couldn't give him what he wanted most.

In a year of conversations, many involving his own death, John never said he expected to be with Walter again. Though he grew up in a churchgoing home and was a choirboy as a child, he did not believe in a next world. "I have no feeling of an afterlife at all," he said. "As a matter of fact, I hope not. I can't imagine anything going on forever. I miss Walter and I wish I could meet him in another life, but I know I won't. Actually, it's rather soothing. It is all going to end; I don't see anything wrong with that." Moving Walter into the next world would be losing him a second time.

Across the elders' varied religious beliefs, none talked about being reunited with loved ones. They'd seen death up close while caring for their partners, and it held no mystery for them. "When you're dead, you're dead," Helen said more than once. Even Fred, who said that heaven was his home, was in no hurry to get there. He preferred life on this plane. "My grandmother used to say, 'That's all right, 'cause one day I'm gonna get to heaven, where the streets are paved with gold, and there'll be honey and milk to drink,' " he said. "And I didn't want to contradict her, but I was thinking, people should try to get something here. Later on I heard that word, 'pie in the sky.' So that's what she was — talking about pie in the sky when she should be talking about having a good life down here on earth."

In each case, the last thing love gave them was a look at what it means to die — its nearness as well as its finality. They accepted that what happened to their spouse would also happen to them. Seeing their future this way stripped away any illusions they might have had about themselves — that they were really some better person waiting to be brought into being, richer, happier, better-looking, thinner, more beloved. Instead, they could look in the mirror and see who they really were; all the future would do was pare them back even further.

Maybe it is a liberty of younger people to think that the best mate is the one you don't have: a stranger you haven't met yet or an improved version of your current partner. It favors the future over the present and past — natural when the future looks long and full of potential, less so when you know what's coming. But it also obscures or diminishes the partner you really have. Ruth, John, and my mother all preferred the satisfactions of the life partners they'd had, whatever their shortcomings, to the unknown. Living in the past may be a cop-out when the future needs you to shape it, but in old age it's a secure place to be. The drive for trading up, wanting the new and improved, may fuel humanity's progress, but it also creates a lot of dissatisfaction and anxiety. The elders had arrested this damage.

They'd also found their way to the essence of love, that it lies in what we give freely, not in tallying what we get in return. We're made better by loving unconditionally: embracing the perfections in our imperfect mate, accepting that they'll never change, growing into our own perfections by loving them. All would rather have had their mates back alive again, of course. But in their loss they had found a resource within themselves. Helen in her relationship with Howie had found the same thing. Happiness wasn't outside themselves, waiting to be born, but within, the thing they already had. It did not depend on Howie or Walter or Ruth's husband or my father. My marital happiness, I came to learn, had never depended on what my wife could give me, and so wasn't undone by whatever I saw as her deficiencies; it was in my hands all along, and in what I could give her.

It took a year with the elders for me to understand this, but once I did, it helped in all my relationships — with my partner, but also with friends, colleagues, and other relatives. Contentment had been there for the grasping, if only I had recognized it. Probably it's there for you. The elders would tell you to grab it while you can, not agitate for something better. They don't have time for delusions, including the delusion that you have time. They're too busy loving like there's no tomorrow, because for any of us, there might not be.

Six:
More Years, Less Life?
"DAY-TO-DAY IT'S PRETTY ROUGH."

The U.S. Census does not paint an inviting picture of our late years. At ages eighty-five and up, one in three people say they have trouble hearing; 31 percent have trouble caring for themselves; half have trouble walking and living independently; and 28 percent say they have cognitive difficulty. Perhaps that's not the payoff you had in mind for all those years of eating quinoa. Heart disease, cancer, diabetes, arthritis, Alzheimer's and other dementias — all increase dramatically by age seventy and accelerate with each additional year. We may be living longer, but as the great gerontologist Sporting Life pointed out, "Who calls dat livin' / When no gal'll give in" to no man whose idea of quality entertainment is a Viagra ad. One thing you could say for saber-toothed tigers or the bubonic plague: they reduced your chances of developing prostate cancer. Let's hear it for whooping cough!

In 1977 a psychologist and epidemiologist named Ernest M. Gruenberg at Johns Hopkins University called the rise of these immiserating diseases the "failures of success": the more the health care system enabled people to survive to old age, the more they developed chronic diseases that sucked the quality out of life. Gruenberg argued that we should view health care as an epidemiological force, like a pathogen, which reduces rates of death but increases rates of sickness and disability. The system's priorities were twisted, Gruenberg believed, because it was preoccupied with extending life, not health. So research dollars went to picking off the acute causes of death, which tend to work pretty quickly, rather than to delaying or preventing chronic diseases that drag on and on, bringing whole families into their circle of pain. To Gruenberg, this went against the oath to do no harm. If cancer patients typically die of pneumonia, say, and we develop treatments for pneumonia, all we've done for their cancer is ensure that they spend more years dying of it. In place of a day on their deathbed, we've given them a month and called it progress.

"Instead of enhancing the people's health this kind of deathly thinking has been increasing the people's sickness and disability," he wrote. "Now that we recognize that our life-saving technology of the past four decades has outstripped our health-preserving technology and that the net effect has been to worsen the people's health, we must begin the search for preventable causes of the chronic illnesses which we have been extending." Yes, medicine was helping us live longer, Gruenberg said, but the extra years were added at the end, when we were too weak or sick to enjoy them.

In part, Gruenberg was reacting to a change in demographics. I knew none of my grandparents; my son knew three of his and there is an outside chance that his children will know one or more of their great-grandparents (nudge, nudge). The U.S. population distribution, which once looked like a pyramid — lots of new children at the base, tapering to a point after age sixty-five or so — now increasingly looks like a rectangle, with a smaller number of babies at the bottom and a larger number of elders living to eighty and beyond. The folks at the top of this box will certainly strain the health care and Social Security systems. Yet there will also be benefits from having an unprecedented number of elders. Some of these are economic — all those healthy, educated, experienced seniors can contribute to the economy in ways that previous cohorts didn't. But just as important is the wisdom they can provide, not only about the past but about the future, for those of us who someday expect to be old ourselves. If we view them only as a liability on the federal balance sheet, we will be squandering a resource we have yet to measure.

Recently, Gruenberg's grim view of longer living got a boost from the oncologist and bioethicist Ezekiel Emanuel, one of the architects of the Obama administration's Affordable Care Act. In a widely circulated essay in *The Atlantic* magazine titled "Why I Hope to Die at 75," Emanuel, who was fifty-seven and robust at the time, argued that living into old age "renders many of us, if not disabled, then faltering and declining, a state that may not be worse than death but is nonetheless deprived. It robs us of our creativity and ability to contribute to work, society, the world. . . . We are no longer remembered as vibrant and engaged but as feeble, ineffectual, even pathetic." Emanuel rejected the surveys that showed old people were happier with their lives, saying polls didn't capture the people in nursing homes or with dementia, who were surely not so happy.

The essay's title was a bit misleading, because Emanuel didn't hope to die at seventy-five; he just didn't want to prolong his life medically beyond that point. So no more cancer screenings, no antibiotics, heart-valve replacement, or bypass surgery. No flu shots, dialysis, step aerobics, or kale salads. If he missed out on some of the rewards of the late years — seeing his grandchildren get older, poker with the fellas, the satisfactions of mentoring the next generation — these were not life's rich bounty but token compensation for the loss of everything that makes life worth living.

The essay sparked heated outcry, not least from seventy-eight-year-olds who didn't appreciate being told it was time to move along. But it also made the valuable point that our national fantasy of living forever, which Emanuel calls the "American immortal," often leads us to squander the years we have. If we knew that the curtain would come down shortly after seventy-five — or that no one would try to stop it once it started to lower — we'd be more inclined to squeeze all the life possible out of the years before then. In his oncology practice, Emanuel said that at some point his patients all described cancer as the best thing that ever happened to them, because it made them concentrate on what was important in life.

This, however, is what many older people do naturally, and a key reason that they are more contented and less stressed. Emanuel's arbitrary cutoff date just forces him to think like a seventy-five-year-old now, without the inconvenience of aging. Alongside the vanity of the American immortal, I would put the vanity of only wanting to live if you can still do all the things you do now. The geriatrician Bill Thomas calls this "the tyranny of *still*": the insistence that old people, unlike everyone else, do not grow or develop, so their goal in life should be to remain exactly as they are or, better yet, regress to an earlier stage. Thomas argues that along with loss there is also gain — in perspective, experience, the accrual of daily pleasures. Instead of dwelling on loss, or clinging desperately to the idea that we *still* play tennis or clean our own house, we can think of aging as a process of change, learning to appreciate rewards as we find them. Loss is one of life's great instillers of wisdom, including the wisdom that finds compensation for the capacities we think we can't live without. Only people in California want it to be sunny every day.

Also, decline is not what it once was. Compared with past generations, Americans are reaching old age with fewer miles on their bodies — less debilitating manual labor, fewer cigarettes, fewer calamitous diseases or infections in early life. So decline is more a relationship or negotiation, with some variation and wiggle room, than a fixed path. Older people now have statins to keep their hearts ticking, cataract surgery to keep the lights on, artificial hips and knees to keep them walking, and swanky scooters to keep them mobile when the new knees go south. Improved fMRI scanning has also revealed that, contrary to decades of medical science, brains continue to develop new neurons throughout life, and that people can increase their number of brain cells the same way they build biceps, through regular exercise.

Three years after Gruenberg diagnosed the failures of success, a Stanford rheumatologist named James F. Fries proposed a much different model of aging. Instead of failures of success, Fries noted *successes* of success. While it was true that medicine and lifestyle changes couldn't eliminate disease and frailty in the elderly, they could delay their onset, compressing the bad stuff into a couple of years at the end. Instead of adding years to the end of life, when everything was falling apart, we were adding them to the middle. He called this effect a "compression of morbidity" and proposed simple ways to enhance it, from reducing obesity and diabetes early in life to replacing failed kidneys or livers later on. Fries has gone on to refine the theory and support it through several long-term studies, and his prescriptions for improving old age have been widely adopted, if not his full paradigm.

In a third model of aging, called "dynamic equilibrium," advances in medicine enable people to bounce back from heart attacks or cancers that previously would have killed them or sent them into grim downward spirals. This model of old age is like Fred's metaphor of the Chesapeake Bay Bridge-Tunnel: you're up for a while, then down, then back up, until finally your clock runs out.

These models of aging have enormous policy implications, especially given the expense of end-of-life care. The ventilator inserted down my father's throat extended his life a few days, but those days were costly and of little value to him — textbook failures of success. On the other hand, after his first heart attack he started walking regularly for exercise and taking medication for his high blood pressure, and he spent his seventies in better health than his sixties — supporting either a compression of morbidity or dynamic equilibrium model.

But whether the last chapter is compressed or drawn out, for everyone, aging happens. Arteries stiffen, joints swell, hair falls out or turns gray, kidneys lose their mojo, and skin doesn't stretch like it used to. Alzheimer's, alas, also sets its own timetable, which medicine has been largely unable to slow down.

Over the course of the year, I saw age's progress in most of the elders. They became more forgetful and less energetic; their aches hurt a little more. Ping's conversation became more disjointed, and her sentences, whether in English or Cantonese, careened off one another at odd angles. "I tell you the truth, everything is enough for me already," she said one day.

But cognitive loss is not a monolithic thing. The brain has many forms of cognition, which involve different regions and are affected differently by aging. Working memory — say, the ability to recall a series of numbers you just heard — diminishes, but long-term memory of your high school years may remain vivid. Those memories have won a Darwinian contest to continue in your brain and won't go easily. We process new information more slowly as we age, and multitasking slows to a crawl. But it is also true that we have less need to process new information, because we aren't exploring new lands or trying to master new technologies. The neurobiologist Elkhonon Goldberg of New York University calls this the "wisdom paradox" and notes that in some useful ways the mind can grow stronger as the brain gets older. "It is time to stop thinking about the aging of our minds and our brains solely in terms of mental losses, and losses alone. The aging of the mind is equally about gains."

Neuroscientists often distinguish between information processing and pattern recognition. These take place in different parts of the brain, and fare differently as we get older. Loosely speaking, processing functions involve the cortex and subcortex, and the right hemisphere, and pattern recognition involves the neocortex and the left hemisphere. Processing information requires a lot of brain energy; recognizing patterns requires relatively little. As we age, we do less of the former and more of the latter.

Instead of seeking out new restaurant experiences, which require us to learn new routes and process new cuisines, we recognize that the bacon at Chez Oeuf is freshest on Saturdays.

Ezekiel Emanuel laments that scientists and artists rarely achieve their great cognitive breakthroughs after their forties, because their brains don't have the firepower needed to forge new solutions to already complicated worlds. Which means that Emanuel at fifty-seven is not likely to concoct wholly novel ways to conceptualize lymphoma or breast cancer. His old cortical and subcortical cells — those responsible for solving complex problems — just won't fire bright enough to light the way.

But his insight that his cancer patients all said that cancer taught them what was important in life arose not from complex processing but from experience and the ability to recognize patterns. He couldn't have made this insight at twenty-five, when the processing centers in his brain were really cooking, because he would not have seen enough patients to recognize the pattern. Yet this insight is arguably as useful to him as any lab breakthrough — it taught him literally how he wanted to live and die. The brain's ability to recognize patterns declines relatively little with age. Older brains also have more templates to work with, because older people simply have more experiences at their disposal. If you lived through the Great Depression, you weren't so shocked when Lehman Brothers melted down.

Helen and Ruth both walked less as the year went on, even though they said walking was one of their great pleasures in life. John had a series of small setbacks, each leaving him a little weaker and more fragile, more dependent on a niece of Walter's named Anne Kornblum, who had become his saintly caregiver. He tore the rotator cuff in his right shoulder and lost most use of the arm — simple surgery for a younger person, but out of the question at his age. When he fell in his kitchen after a couple of sleepless nights, it raised the prospect that the next fall would send him to a nursing home, which he feared more than death. Then, in October, he had a urinary tract infection and needed antibiotics, and the complication of remembering one more prescription was too much for him: he ended up taking three days' worth on the first day. At the urology clinic, where he waited more than an hour to be seen, he told the urologist that he thought of killing himself.

"I can't stab myself," he said.

"Don't want to do that," the doctor said.

"And I can't jump out the window because I can't get the gate open. And I probably wouldn't die because I'm on too low a floor. The problem is I'm too healthy to die."

At home afterward, sitting with Anne, he dropped his talk of suicide. Anne works as a criminal investigator for the U.S. Postal Service, and is not someone you can bullshit. In his own apartment, John's theatrical despair gave way to fatigue. He had ventured out and made it home one more time, but now he was worn out.

"I have moments of great pleasure," he said. "But day-to-day it's pretty rough."

Fred Jones had the hardest year. He was the youngest of the six but ate an unhealthy diet and had a history of heart problems. He'd started the year with an infection that made his right foot look like something out of a battlefield triage unit. To reach his apartment, he had to climb the three flights of stairs half a flight at a time, pausing to rest at each landing. Sometimes his good leg hurt more than the infected one. "Coming up those steps, it was almost like somebody was squeezing my back together," he said. "And then after a while it radiated down the leg, where I feel like something's biting me on the leg and the knee and the thigh and the back and the upper arm. It's all over."

Over the years, he'd often told himself he should move to a building with an elevator, but his rent was just three hundred dollars a month, so he always figured a way to stick it out for just a little longer. Now his home was ill-matched to his body, and with his neighborhood becoming gentrified, apartments like his were going for five times what he paid, even without an elevator. So he steeled himself to manage the stairs, and at the end of each day peeled off a sock caked with blood and pus. It was a rotten trade-off and Fred was smart enough to know it. "When you get hung up between cheap rent in a bad place and expensive rent in a better place, you say, 'This is not that good, but I've been here for certain years,' and I keep talking myself into staying there," he said. He really needed a home care nurse to help him dress the infection and an aide to help manage the apartment. But Fred was in what is known as the hole in the health care donut. He'd worked for the city and had a pension of two thousand dollars a month, plus another thousand dollars in Social Security benefits. But this meant he wasn't eligible for social assistance to help pay for the services he increasingly needed, let alone a subsidized apartment in an elevator building. It was a situation that couldn't last, I thought, but Fred never seemed discouraged. As long as he woke up in the morning, it was another good day.

Then in May I called him and got a message saying the phone had been temporarily disconnected at the customer's request. I called the hospital affiliated with his podiatrist, then the one he'd been in the year before with low blood pressure, then all the hospitals in Brooklyn. Nada. None had a patient named Frederick Jones. In all of Brooklyn, no Fred Jones? The agency that delivered his meals on wheels told me that he was alive, that he had called to stop delivery, but under privacy laws could not tell me more. I kept calling the hospitals, figuring that he would eventually emerge. Finally a hospital acknowledged that yes, it had a patient named Frederick Jones, in the geriatrics unit.

Fred was smiling when I got to his room, explaining that surgeons had amputated parts of two toes because of gangrene. The pain from the operation was "excruciating," he said, but he didn't want morphine because he associated it with addiction. He

141

had been taken to the hospital ER directly from his primary care doctor's office, so he didn't have a change of clothes or his phone book; he couldn't even tell friends or neighbors where he was. He didn't know when he would get home, or what sort of bills would pile up in his absence. He notified the electric company and credit card companies that he might not pay his bills for a while.

From another room a woman's voice shouted, "No no, don't die, please don't die. See, I knew this was going to happen."

At one time Fred's infection, if he had lived long enough to develop it, would have carried him off. Maybe in the future the diabetes underlying it will be fully curable — doctors will have patients like Fred bounding up their apartment stairs like young bunnies. But for now Fred's problems put him in a somatic turf war in which the most he could hope was to slow the enemy's advance. Quickly or slowly, he was losing ground he once controlled. In the prior year he had spent sixty-four days in the hospital or rehab for low blood pressure. Now he was in for an even longer spell. Watching him try to walk just a few steps over the next month, visibly in pain, I didn't see how he could ever return to his walk-up apartment. The days without walking were causing both legs to atrophy. His doctors didn't seem to appreciate his situation. "They told me I'm going to need a walker," he said. "I have a walker. In fact, I got three of them. But I can't manage to get it up and down three flights of steps."

Fred was the problem that the health care system — the part of it that pays the bills, anyway — worries about. Gruenberg developed his "failures of success" paradigm in 1977, just twelve years after Lyndon Johnson signed H.R. 6675, establishing Medicare as the safety net for an economically vulnerable population. The system was perfect as long as it didn't encounter seniors like Fred, who faced limited prospects and unlimited bills. After he was moved to a nursing home for rehab, he had no incentive to leave as the bills ran up; to the contrary, as long as he was there his most expensive bills were the ones fully covered.

One day at the nursing home, I asked him what young people should know about old age. The question seemed to puzzle him: old age was just a season of life like any other. Today was not much different from yesterday, and tomorrow would not be much different from today. "Except for the difficulty in buttoning my clothes or bend-ing over and getting back pains from tying my shoes or something like that, or looking in the mirror and seeing gray hairs — all those things are not surprising," he said. "You know they're coming, and this is a process of life. Just go from one age to another. I don't see a particular different feeling."

Fred, unlike me, never doubted that he would get back to his apartment — never lost interest in seeing the morrow, never considered at what point life would not be worth living. Life was life, whether in a nursing home bed or in a Jacuzzi filled with hundred-dollar bills and million-dollar starlets. The health problems that looked so dire to me were just what he was used to. You lived your life around your circumstances. He had grown up poor in Norfolk, Virginia, and lost his father to a burst appendix before he turned three. In his childhood he had seen his grandmother and mother face poverty and racism that exceeded whatever he would experience. Adjusting to life in all its trials, for Fred, was what living was about. He had surpassed expectations by going to Virginia State University on the GI Bill, the first in his family to attend college, and was beating the odds just by breathing at eighty-eight.

"I don't know anybody my age," he said. "Most friends I had on my job passed on. I have to be realistic. I know we're not here forever, so I try to just take one day at a time and enjoy it. Of course I ask God for a hundred and ten, a hundred and fifteen years. I might get there. I don't know what heaven is like, but I know that I like what I have down here. And I like the old statement, 'Heaven is my home, but I'm not homesick.' I want to stay here and enjoy life."

We were in the dining room at the nursing home, where Fred was wearing clothes provided to him by the staff; he had long since lost track of the one set of clothes he had worn to the hospital a month prior. His hair was turning gray at the roots without his regular dye jobs, and someone had shaved his mustache without consulting him. "I don't know what I'm wearing," he said. "This might be a dead man's outfit. I guess they save clothes. I don't know where they get them from." For someone as un-regimented as Fred, the nursing home's strict schedule was a jolt to the system. He ate all his meals in the same seat with the same people. That morning he'd slept late, so the staff didn't take him to brush his teeth.

Like all the elders, Fred worked hard to maintain his autonomy, a battle that got more challenging each year. But instead of complaining about the home's strict regimen, he took it in stride, finding pleasures in the company there. He made friends with residents and staff members, and went to services with his roommate, a Jehovah's Witness. He sang Billy Eckstine's "I Apologize" at karaoke day. Instead of mourning his lost toes, he looked forward to getting home, thinking about "all the good life I'm missing out on," even if it meant hobbling up the stairs to an apartment that was in shambles. "It's close to a dump, but I'm accustomed to being there," he said. I left the nursing home filled with the joy of living.

Fred's attitude toward his late years was that they weren't as good as his younger years, but only in the sense that a small bag of potato chips isn't as good as a big bag. They're still potato chips. And besides, what else was he going to do with his time, if not live it? The alternative was death, which was no potato chips at all. "My favorite part of the day is waking up in the morning and thanking God for another day," he said, beaming at the words coming out of his mouth. "That's my favorite part of the day."

Old age ain't no place for sissies, goes the cliché attributed to Bette Davis. But this is exactly wrong. Old age is for sissies — eventually it's for almost everyone, thanks to modern medicine and sanitation. Whether its assault on the body is compressed or elongated, at some point anyone who lives a long time is going to have an aging body.

But what is old age? To a great extent we've made it a verdict, something that happens to people who didn't have the good sense to take up yoga before it was too late, meaning roughly their twenties. Which is to say, old age is a concept largely defined by the people who have never lived it. People in the middle third of life, described self-servingly as life's prime, have managed to discount the perspective of younger people as youthful folly and that of older people as senile nattering.

My relationship with my mother illustrated the differences in the ways old people and their youngers view old age. She refused to exercise or lose weight, even though this was the one thing that gave her any lasting relief from her chronic back pain. Physical therapy, she said, was "hype." Though her building had an indoor pool, she didn't swim because it hurt too much to change into a bathing suit. Tai chi classes, at 10:00 a.m., were too early in the morning. As the pain in her back and legs grew, my brothers and I discouraged her from getting a motorized wheelchair. Once she stopped walking, I argued, she'd stop exercising her lungs, which would take its toll throughout her body.

But I was wrong. The wheelchair liberated her and enabled her to go to museums and plays, often at a discount. Here was a lesson in acceptance and adaptation. In a culture that constantly tells us to overcome our limitations, sometimes it is more productive to find ways to live with them. For people on short time, short-term fixes — or acceptance — are sometimes the best answer. And we're all on short time; older people just understand this more viscerally.

During my year of visits Helen progressed from a cane to a walker, but didn't think of herself as being over-the-hill — over-the-hill was the nursing home residents who had dementia. She never wanted to be one of them. Ruth, similarly, no longer walked as she once had, but took satisfaction in not being in a wheelchair or losing her mental faculties. Of course life was worth living.

Fred couldn't wait to wake up again tomorrow morning, a day older and frailer, but still himself. With the exception of John, all seemed to redraw the line between what was acceptable and what was too much, pushing it just past their level of disability. Health problems that looked devastating to me looked to them like a part of life's progress after eighty-five — what was truly bad was always a step down the road.

Instead of idealizing their younger selves, each of the elders focused on the things that made them most themselves — meaning what made them most human. For Jonas it was making art; for Helen it was Howie. Ruth, who hated being displaced from her old home, strengthened ties with her children and extended family, learning to use e-mail and Facebook to keep up. John revisited memories of Walter, and Ping maintained a tight mah-jongg group. For Fred, every day was a gift, every moment a chance to be happy. "Like the game [on TV] last night," he said. "For a few minutes I didn't think of nothing but the game. I jumped up, man, good I don't have no wife in the bed, she think I'm crazy, jumping up out of the bed like that. In the moment, that's the happiness. I think sadness is when you're concentrated on one particular bad incident that's happened."

At first, these compensations seemed paltry compared with what they had given up. But over the year I learned otherwise: the compensations were big enough to fill their lives. If they didn't choose the conditions their bodies were in, none of us does at any age. They saw themselves as sums not of their disabilities but of their strategies for living with them. I remembered my father's last days, in a miserable Newark hospital room, hooked up to machines that prolonged his life. That, surely, was a life not worth living, and certainly not one anyone would want. But in his mind he went to pleasant chapters of his life he'd never shared before, maybe because he hadn't needed them when he was healthy. What the elders had discovered, I began to see, was not just a preparation for death but a prescription for life at any age.

My visits became seminars less in aging than in living. Difficulties in my life, including my divorce and a torn ligament in my foot that put me in a walking boot, no longer ate at me. Visits with my mother, too, became more pleasant and invigorating. Each elder had different lessons to teach: from Fred, the power of gratitude; from Ping, the choice to be happy; from John, acceptance of death; from Helen, learning to love and be needed; from Jonas, living with purpose; and from Ruth, nourishing the people who matter. For centuries societies had relied on elders for these lessons and more. It was only in recent times that this wisdom went unheard. I wasn't blazing new ground, but rediscovering some ancient connections. The blazing part was how happy the lessons made me, and how I wished I'd learned them earlier.

■ ■ ■ ■

PART II
THE LESSONS

■ ■ ■ ■

SEVEN:
THE LESSONS OF FRED

"I SAY, THANK GOD FOR ANOTHER DAY, ON MY WAY TO 110."

My purpose is to live, be happy, enjoy life, talking. Have a good time with friends. Go to church on Sunday. Associate, go out to dinner once in a while. And the days will go by fast.

— Frederick Jones, eighty-eight

Visits with Fred were always an education. He talked about wanting to go to Red Lobster, where he used to take dates, and about avoiding a nearby street because there was a funeral home on it. He told me about an ex-girlfriend who "liked the lollipop," and showed me composition books filled with handwritten song lyrics or words of wisdom that he wanted to remember. The price of silk ties at Bloomingdale's, dancing at the Savoy Ballroom in Harlem on Sunday afternoons — Fred's past was a tray of bonbons he never tired of sampling. One day he found a large envelope stuffed with various medications, all expired. Whether

155

he had replaced the medications or just not taken them he could not be sure.

"Listen to this one," he said, thumbing through one of the composition books. " 'Don't let your environment limit your vision.' That's Joel Osteen." Fred watched Joel Osteen every Sunday, especially since he stopped going to church. He admired Osteen's full head of hair and his pretty wife. He paused to consider the words, then read them aloud again. The next aphorism was from a source he did not know. " 'Sacrifice is the supreme act of love,' " he read.

Did he agree with that? I asked.

"Well," he said, "depends on how much I got to sacrifice." He didn't need to wink. With Fred, that was a given.

Fred had his toe surgery on May 29, was transferred to the nursing home for rehab on June 8, and in mid-August was told to prepare for his discharge. In the vacuum of information that is a patient's life, it felt to Fred like he was being hurried out for financial reasons. "My HIP insurance called the nursing home and told them that I've had enough time there, they weren't paying any more," he said. He had gone through the same thing eight months earlier, at a different nursing home. "So now I either have to pay myself, apply for Medicaid, which I'm not eligible for, or leave." On August 28, after three months away, he returned home.

In his apartment four days later, he was tired, nauseous, and in a lot of pain, complaining that he was discharged too early. His discharge sheet read:

Mr. Jones will continue independence with getting out of bed, transfer from chair to bed and walking using a rolling walker. Mr. Jones will require supervision with bathing. He needs assist with meal preparation, cleaning and laundry. He is independent with toileting and dressing. He will maintain daily recreational activities with discharge to community. He will be discharged to community with visiting nurse service. Resident will be using Medicare hours. Resident has active meals on wheels and Express Scripts in place. Family is involved and supportive.

Some of this was correct. The nursing home had sent him home with a walker to go with the three he already had, but unless he suddenly learned to carry it up and down the stairs, it wouldn't get him very far. The home health aide had still not arrived, despite assurances. His daughter was indeed involved and supportive, but she was too sick to do much more than buy him a few groceries on his first day back. He was doing his best to navigate a system that is opaque even to people with energy and a degree in health care administration. He had neither.

Fred was in his pajamas, unshaven, the closest I'd seen him to being down. He hadn't eaten much since getting home. The nursing home hadn't dyed his hair, so he was completely gray for the first time since he started coloring it twenty years before. His reflection scared him.

"I really feel like going back, but they're not going to accept me back," he said. "A friend of mine is telling me the way to get back is call an ambulance, go to the hospital, and then when they discharge me they'll discharge me to another health-related facility. But I'm tired of these health-related facilities anyway, and the hospital. So I guess I just do whatever I can."

We talked some more, but Fred didn't have the energy for it. I'd brought him some Chinese food, enough to last a few days, and he ate gingerly, thanking me not just for the food but for the gesture. In the nursing home, at least he'd had people to talk to and regular meals to build up his strength.

He'd gained a little weight and raised his blood pressure, which sometimes ran dangerously low. But he'd had no privacy or freedom to set his own hours. Now he was back to staying up late and only eating when he felt like preparing food. He tried to be upbeat about going out again, but for once there didn't seem to be any oomph behind it. "I don't know," he said. "I'm taking my time because I just don't feel like it. I don't even feel like putting my clothes on."

The remarkable thing about Fred was not that he felt this way, but that it didn't last. I had included Fred in the group of elders because he was someone whose life had clearly taken a turn for the worse, an isolated old man with a bad heart and declining mobility. Yet Fred never saw himself that way. He was thankful for the gift of another day, for a visitor, for a hot meal, for a sunny afternoon he couldn't go out to enjoy. More than almost anyone I've met, Fred lived in the moment, in gratitude for the pleasures he could still enjoy. The pains, he insisted, were temporary. He didn't worry about tomorrow, except to the extent of wanting to be around to enjoy it. I'd sit with him and feel petty for not appreciating the things that I had.

Then, in midyear, I started trying to follow Fred's lead: instead of stewing over my complaints, I began to consciously give thanks for things I took for granted. My comforts were so extravagant compared with Fred's; how could I be less grateful? I started with the easy stuff: the love from my parents or girlfriend, time with my friends, the good fortune of my job. This set off a second, less obvious train of thought. Being grateful meant acknowledging the benign forces in the universe that were working in my favor. Life wasn't just a battle I had to fight on my own: it was also a bounty I was lucky to receive, hands I was lucky to have supporting me. Gradually, I began to understand gratitude the way Fred saw it, less as a reaction to this or that circumstance than as a way of looking at the world. Life itself was reason to give thanks. In this light, it made sense that he was grateful, even if others would hope that Fred's life didn't happen to them. Soon I was returning to his apartment for another hit of what he was smoking, because it was making my life better. It beat being anxious or depressed or disappointed.

A week or so after he got out of the nursing home, he was back to his upbeat self, walking partway down the stairs and back up again, looking forward to feeling even better in the coming days. He was still working on the leftover Chinese food. The worst had passed, as it had always done in his life, and things were only getting better. To live in the moment was to relish each stair he was able to climb today. One hundred and ten years still looked good to him — at the rate he was improving, why not? He took a moment to give thanks for his fortunes, modest as they were. "With God's help," he said, "I'll be able to get out next week."

Fred Jones was born in Philadelphia in 1927, when the life expectancy for African American males was under fifty. After his father died when Fred was two and a half, his mother and grandmother worked menial jobs to support him and his older brother. His mother was a seamstress earning twenty-five dollars a week; his grandmother cleaned houses. He grew up beguiled by the mysteries of sex, and remained so in his old age. Before we'd even met in person, he told me about women who were shamelessly maneuvering to get in bed with him — a favorite topic of conversation, it turned out.

"I don't really know what it means to be in love," he said one day in his apartment, sitting amid the accumulations of a lifetime. A television that barely worked rested on one that didn't work at all; a bicycle that he hadn't ridden since 1967 vied for space with old religious pamphlets, insurance offers, and photographs still in the envelopes from the drugstore. "I mean, I love my brother. I like women, I like being with them, but I've never really been in love, where you forget about everything else. With a girlfriend, it's here today and gone tomorrow."

He had a photo of a woman on the refrigerator, but he had stopped calling her long ago, he said, around the time she started talking about marriage. He cared more about a photo in his bedroom, this one of his mother. The picture, curling at the edges, showed an attractive middle-aged woman with a firm smile and neatly curled hair, the same wide brow as Fred's, younger than Fred when I met him. Her dress might have been her Sunday best.

"It's good I live alone, because somebody would think I'm crazy," he said. "I stand right there and talk to her. Oh, 'I love you and I appreciate all the things you did for us, and when I was a kid I didn't know I was poor because we always had nice toys for Christmas and decent clothes to wear to school.' Just reminiscing. I go through all that stuff."

The saddest time of his life, he said, was

162

when his mother died in 1979. He had left her alive in her hospital bed that afternoon, then gone to a movie at the mall nearby — *Heaven Can Wait,* as it happened. The next morning when he returned to her room, he found her mattress rolled up. "I knew what that meant," he said. "I got so weak in the knees. I haven't been to the movies since." Since that day, he said, "I think about it and have long dreams about her, but she always disappears."

If there is a starting point for Fred's sense of gratitude, it lies in his childhood and the care of his mother and grandmother. Many of his stories, those not involving sex, led back to these women and the hard lives they led, the sacrifices they made for him and his older brother. After his mother lost her job during the Depression, Fred remembered a house so cold they all huddled near the potbelly stove that warmed only part of one room; food came from a charity pantry. But these were not unhappy memories. "When you're a kid," he said, "if you're with your parents, and your parents are doing the best they can for you, even though you may be very poor, you're happy, because that's all you know."

Even so, he said, "I didn't even know I was poor until I got to seventeen, eighteen years old, and I started reading about the Rockefellers and the Kennedys and people like that with all the bread. We had Christmas toys, we had clothes, we had little shoe pennies for school. I could get a six-pack of glazed donuts from a day-old store for ten cents. That was my lunch." The experience taught him early on that problems were only problems if you thought about them that way. Otherwise they were life — and yours for the living.

Later on, after he served in the military and then went to college on the GI Bill, his big regret was not being able to return his grandmother's kindness. With his first paycheck, he said, he planned to gather all the underwear that his grandmother made for herself, "find me the biggest garbage can and put all that stuff in it. My first two hundred dollars I'm going to spend on her. But she died a year before I graduated from college, so I missed out on that. Then I started sending my mother money every month."

The miracle of Fred was that with all his hardships, he always found reasons to feel fortunate. He was buffeted one way or another by the health care system, racked with pain, each day a little more isolated from the outside world. His daughter was dying and he was largely estranged from his other five children. His brother, the closest person in his life, hit his head in a fall and was having seizures that affected his speech, so the brothers could no longer talk on the phone. Fred took it all in stride. "Life is pretty good," he said one day in the nursing home.

Here was a lesson in giving up the myth of control. If you believe you are in control of your life, steering it in a course of your choosing, then old age is an affront, because it is a destination you didn't choose. But if you think of life instead as an improvisation in response to the stream of events coming at you — that is, a response to the world as it is — then old age is more another chapter in a long-running story. The events are different, but they're always different, and always some seem too much to bear.

I was sure Fred would not be able to stay in his apartment. He seemed almost reckless in his refusal to face the situation. This was the flip side of Fred's focus on the present: he didn't plan for the future. He could have moderated his diabetes by cutting out the ice cream and Pringles; he could have thought practically about finding another home, one without stairs to climb. He wouldn't think that way. Now that he was home, it seemed clear that he couldn't take care of himself. His good cheer was fine, but it wouldn't carry his body up and down the thirty-seven steps.

But after a couple of weeks, he made his way down the stairs and walked on his own to the store, even crossing a busy avenue without a traffic light. By October we went for a long walk together, at his insistence, even though I offered him a ride. It was a spectacular Indian summer afternoon and Fred wore a checked wool sport jacket and crimson knit shirt along with his orthopedic shoes. He was a little behind in his laundry — maybe a couple of years — so he didn't have the maroon socks he would have wanted to go with the red shirt, or a hand-kerchief for his breast pocket, but you could tell he felt happy to be out and on his own feet. The gloom of his first days back home was long gone.

"I never wanted to act like old people," he said. "They sit around, 'Oh, child, I could tell it was going to rain 'cause my lumbago is bothering me.' I don't see no enjoyment in talking about illnesses. I like to talk about stuff like songs and who wrote them, and the football game on Sunday. That's upbeat stuff to me. But people are like, 'Oh, last night I heard a noise, I thought someone

166

was at the door, someone was breaking in.'
I don't want to hear that kind of stuff. I
know it happens, but it doesn't do anything
for my spirits."

He sang, in his best Billy Eckstine:

Jelly jelly jelly
Jelly stays on my mind

"You know that one?" he said.

After one of the newspaper articles, three
readers got in touch with Fred. One wanted
to come pray with him, another to look in
on him because he seemed isolated. Fred
encouraged both. The third, a retired execu-
tive named Jim Healy, took Fred to lunch
at the Burger King near his apartment, and
afterward asked Fred what he would do if
he found a couple of hundred dollars on
the street.

Buy a suit, Fred said.

So they did.

Fred fancied something in purple, which
complicated the shopping a little, but he
had spent years looking in windows, so he
knew where to go. When it came to haber-
dashery, Fred had inherited his mother's
love of color. By his count, he once owned
eighty-three pairs of socks, twenty-five belts,
and ten or fifteen handkerchiefs, all stuffed

167

into shopping bags after his last live-in girlfriend moved out and took the dresser with her.

The purple suit was double-breasted and checked, and Fred looked great in it. He was a lion in winter, maybe autumn, even. His smile made my year. Jim Healy, when we talked, was as elated as Fred was, and as grateful. Like me, he knew that he was getting as much as he gave.

That was how things went with Fred. He never stayed down, never worried about the future — about things that hadn't happened — and never lost his sense of wonder at the world he'd been born into. Of course there was a purple suit. The world was full of gifts. Even on hard days, he liked to revel in memories of sweeter ones.

"Man, the Easter Parade isn't like it used to be," he said one day, another bonbon plucked out of the box. This was after I showed him a cell phone video of a second line parade from New Orleans, featuring a woman rolling her ample backside. "I remember a woman with a live little chickadee attached to her hat in some way, and he was going cheep cheep," Fred said. "I thought, man, they really turn it on." It was typical of Fred. He'd suddenly remember something funny or kind or just peculiar, and his whole body would seem more alive. A live chickadee on a hat? Why not? Another day it was the sailors in Norfolk, Virginia, who tipped him to steer them to prostitutes when he was just sixteen. Or the perils of fellow travelers on the sea of love. These were some of his favorite memories. "I remember the '21' Club, this woman got out of a limousine, looked like it was as long as this room," he said. "She had a fur. I don't know what it cost but it looked good. And she had it partially dragging on the ground. She was already tanked up from wherever she came from, and she's going into '21.' It was two women and one man. I said, boy, you really got troubles on your hands. Two half-drunk women? That's too much."

Fred never blamed anyone for his hardships. He had made a mess of his life, but it was his mess, so his good fortune to live it. It beat living someone else's mess. Even the loss of sex was just one more thing for him to adjust to. The art of living, after all, lies in living the life you have, in the body that you have. Sex was still a part of Fred's life; it just shifted to the organ of memory and imagination. "I don't miss it," he said. "I feel like I had more than my share. I don't like to brag." He pointed to his noggin, indicating that Elvis had not left the building, just moved to another floor. "It's all here now," he said. "That's the thing. That's the difference. I say now, the boy don't want to raise his head."

He had learned to curb a temper that his brother once said would land him in jail, and learned to live with his allergies to commitment. These were threads in his life's story, and his life was a gift he had gotten for free. Whatever vices or bad habits he had — and he was too cheap to drink or gamble — were just more opportunities for God to show love and forgiveness. "When I say my prayers, that's asking God to make me a better person this year than I was last year," he said. "You got children growing up here and there, you can't be too good a papa. So I guess they just don't feel like coming to see me. That's the way that goes."

Christianity, Judaism, Islam, Buddhism, Hinduism, and a pile of self-help books all extol the virtues of gratitude. Cicero called it "not only the greatest of virtues, but the parent of all the others." G. K. Chesterton wrote that "thanks are the highest form of thought, and . . . gratitude is happiness doubled by wonder," and made a habit of saying grace not just before meals, but "before the play and the opera, and grace before the concert and the pantomime, and grace before I open a book, and grace before sketching, painting, swimming, fencing, boxing, walking, playing, dancing and grace before I dip the pen in the ink."

Almost everyone is grateful some of the time, especially when we hope for something in return. You thank the host for a lovely dinner in hopes of getting invited to the next one. Gratitude at its most basic is a social sweetener. People who acknowledge the kindnesses of others are more pleasant to be around, and so attract more kindnesses. Whereas nobody likes an ingrate.

But some people are grateful seemingly as their default state, even when no one's looking. Their lives aren't necessarily better than other people's, but they find more reasons to give thanks for their small rewards. Fred Jones was one of those people. Giving thanks made him happy, which made him grateful, which made him happy.

In 2015, researchers at the University of Southern California set out to study what happens in the brain of a person feeling gratitude. Using fMRI scanners, they gave twenty-three subjects very short texts written by Holocaust survivors describing acts of kindness they received from strangers, and asked them to imagine themselves in the position of the people receiving the favors. Some of the gifts were quite small, like a loaf of stale bread; others involved great sacrifice and risk, like a hiding place when Nazi troops were closing in. The subjects were asked to rate how thankful they were for the gifts. The researchers then mapped the regions of the brain activated.

The scans showed activity in multiple parts of the brain, suggesting that gratitude involved a network of emotional responses, even when the favors were small. The subjects' brains lit up not just in their reward centers, commensurate with the benefit they received, but also their moral and social processing centers, responding to the persons giving the gifts. The more grateful the subjects said they were, the stronger the response in the regions of their brains governing moral and social cognition. This was often unrelated to the size of the favor. Gratitude, as the subjects experienced it, entailed a relationship with others, not just with the benefit received.

The implications of this are fascinating. If a marketer says to you, "We'd like your opinion of a new product we're introducing in your area," and hands you an insanely delicious piece of pie, your reward centers will fire like roman candles, but your moral and social processing centers probably won't. You respond to the pie, not the person giving it. But if a neighbor offers the same pie, it'll light up all the regions. This will hold even if the neighbor's pie is half the size, or not as tasty. Gratitude doesn't depend on the thing you're grateful for as much as your acknowledgment of the giver. Someone disinclined toward gratitude might receive the neighbor's gift without much response in the social and moral processing centers.

The experiment also illustrates how gratitude can accompany suffering. You don't have to be on easy street to feel grateful. No one would envy a Holocaust refugee huddled over a loaf of stale bread, except for a refugee without one. A hard life may have as many opportunities for gratitude as a cushy one.

It was easy to see this in Fred, who had plenty of reasons to dwell on his problems but didn't. In giving thanks for even small pleasures — a scoop of ice cream, a smile from a neighbor — he magnified these pleasures and left less room for complaint or envy. Giving thanks also tempered his isolation, because it connected him mentally with forces beyond himself. He saw the world as a benevolent place that wanted him to be happy, an extraordinary mind-set for an African American man raised poor in the South. At times I worried I was making the mistake of the young Mark Twain, who preposterously asked an enslaved family servant, "How is it that you've lived sixty years and never had any trouble?" only to have her school him in the sorrows of her days. But Fred was always candid about his hardships. He just didn't define his life by them.

Often during the year I asked him how he did it. The question never seemed to make sense to him; the things he was thankful for were so simple and accessible that enjoying them was no more difficult than breathing. His faith was part of the bargain, of course, but it seemed more a way of organizing his positive emotions than the force driving them. He didn't want a life other than the one he had. "My purpose is to live, be happy, enjoy life, talking," he said. "Have a good time with friends. Go to church on Sunday. Associate, go out to dinner once in a while. And the days will go by fast."

It was also easy to see how this contentment and gratitude eluded my mother. Though her life was more comfortable than

Fred's, they had different expectations of the coming days. Fred's life experience taught him that the worst hardships were temporary, so he didn't spend his days thinking about them. This was the optimism of my father, who believed that the world was getting better, and that "sickness" was just another word for something human genius would someday eliminate. My mother, whose hardship was chronic back pain, knew that it would only get worse, and spent a lot of energy chasing treatments that mostly disappointed her. Fred took to physical therapy with confidence that he would walk the stairs again; my mother resisted in the knowledge that her back pain only increased.

Robert A. Emmons, a psychology professor at the University of California, Davis, has for most of this century studied the positive effects of gratitude in people like Fred, and ways to instill these in people who aren't constitutionally grateful. Back in 2003, he and Michael E. McCullough of the University of Miami set out to measure whether giving thanks changed people's attitudes toward life, or whether people with positive outlooks just tended to be more grateful. In a series of experiments of different durations and intensities, they asked subjects to keep journals of things they were grateful for (one group of subjects) or things that annoyed or bothered them (a second group). A third group was asked to write down something that happened to them or some way in which they were better off than others. In each experiment, the three groups began with comparable levels of gratitude. The subjects in two experiments were university students; in one they were people with neuromuscular diseases. The experiments ran from two weeks to nine weeks.

In each study, the subjects who wrote down something they were grateful for reported greater levels of well-being and more optimism about the coming weeks or days. The more often they wrote, the stronger the effect. Depending on how the study was constructed, they reported other positive effects: they exercised more, slept better, woke up more refreshed, or were more likely to have helped someone else with a problem. In later experiments, Emmons and others have found that people who gave thanks had lower blood pressure, less inflammation, better immune function, and lower levels of the stress hormone cortisol.

One finding from the 2003 studies was that just writing down ways in which one is better off than others did not produce the same benefits. It was not enough to be conscious of one's advantages; one had to be grateful for them. Fred, who had more hardships than most people but was highly grateful, wanted to live to 110; my mother, who had more advantages than most people, saw no point in living. Advantages alone — even awareness of them — weren't enough, perhaps because they can be lost. Gratitude, on the other hand, was an affirmation that the world gave you things, and might continue to do so.

Here is the kind of line that always made Fred happy: "My wife never cheated on me," he said. "Because I never had a wife." His whole face lit up and he chuckled gently. We were in his apartment in early December, and he was feeling sated from Thanksgiving leftovers brought to him by his daughter. It was starting to get cold outside, and the apartment, sealed year-round against the climate and poor services from the landlord, was stuffy and cool. The music on his mind was "Coochi-Coochi-Coo" by Ella Fitzgerald, "Prisoner of Love" by Russ Columbo (a particularly lush and romantic version of this song), and "Body and Soul" by Coleman Hawkins. Fred remembered dancing to Hawkins's big band at the Savoy Ballroom. "Oh man, he plays a solo on the tenor sax, beautiful," Fred said. We were nearing the end of our year together, an occasion for reflection, so I asked him about his youth, and what he had expected of old age when he was younger.

His answer was pure Fred. "One day at a time, dear Lord, one day at a time," he said. "I didn't think no further than today. Then tomorrow I think of that day and that's it."

In retrospect, you could trace many of Fred's hardships to this attitude. Yet he didn't. Instead he focused on the pleasures that he still enjoyed. So many of the people he had worked with or befriended were dead, unable to enjoy a sunny day or the arrival of a Social Security check, but he was still kicking, whatever his infirmities. Life on earth wasn't supposed to be perfect; it was just supposed to be life — miracle enough when you thought about it.

"I don't know of any other place," he said. "There's so much in the world to keep me happy while I'm here. Now, after a hundred and ten–plus years — I want those to be in good health. If I need someone to cook for me, fine. But I like to get my shower and put my clothes on and comb my hair. I don't have any desires other than to do things I enjoy, like window-shop."

178

Fred grew quiet. It was close to the shortest day of the year, and the streetlight outside cast sideways shadows into the living room. We were in one of those awkward male silences: neither of us wanted to say anything gooey, but we also didn't want to say goodbye. Of the elders, Fred had been the hardest to convince and the quickest to confide, and there were still corners of his life he didn't want to lay open. I asked what he looked forward to in the coming year. Looking ahead was always a challenge for Fred, maybe because each year brought problems he didn't need.

"Next year?" he said. "To be eighty-nine years old the entire year, until 2017 in March, when I'll be looking forward to being ninety." He chuckled. He had known dirt streets in Norfolk as a child, and even now liked to swing his cane in front of him like the flashy moonshiners of his youth. He hoped to be a better person in the next year, he said, but he didn't count on it. "I don't make no resolutions," he said. "I can't keep them."

He had begun the year in a nursing home for his first rehab, so in one sense he was ending it better than he started. But he was a dying man and smart enough to know it. He just didn't choose to look at his life that

179

way. Maybe this was a defense mechanism, the way his talk of sex glossed over his self-doubts as a father and partner, but it pushed him through his days, and gave a name and place to his joy. On one of my last visits with Fred, parts of his apartment were in near-darkness because he couldn't climb a ladder to change the lightbulbs. In the kitchen he could no longer raise his arm high enough to reach the cord to turn on the light there. An old man alone in the dark — that was the story I'd set out to report a year earlier. Now it didn't seem so revelatory. His life was so much more interesting than that. I changed the bulbs for him and lengthened the cord in the kitchen. It was a breach of journalist protocol — report the news, don't make it — but I figured the ghosts of Edward R. Murrow and others would forgive me. They were old men or women, too, before they became legends.

Fred took the help without embarrassment. He was as rickety as his apartment, but at least he had light. Whether he would live to see those new bulbs need changing was anyone's guess, but in their bright glow he was willing to say he would. That was Fred. Maybe it was time to start missing him already. "What do they say about the Timex watch?" he said. "It took a licking but it kept on ticking." It wasn't Joel Osteen, but it would do. "That's how I feel. I've taken some lickings but thank God I'm still ticking. Yes indeed."

Eight:
The Lessons of Ping

"I'M OLDER, I HAVE TO MAKE MYSELF FEEL GOOD."

We never talk about dying. What's the use? When you get old you have to die. We go downstairs and play cards. At our age, you should prepare yourself.
— Ping Wong, ninety

Compared with Fred, who had done everything to reach old age financially secure, Ping Wong had almost nothing. She spent her working years earning below minimum wage in a doctor's office in Chinatown, and retired at close to eighty with no savings, relying on Supplemental Security benefits of just seven hundred dollars a month. Three decades after moving to the United States from Hong Kong, she still spoke only rudimentary English. Her husband and two of her sisters were dead, and her only son had been murdered in a department store in Canton, China. Even after two hip replacement operations, the arthritis in her

182

back and legs made it painful for her to walk.

When I met her in her well-kept apartment near Gramercy Park, she had only one complaint: old people who complained too much.

"People complain about their health, or they say, today I have to see the doctor," she said. "Many of them are like that. Most of them, to tell you the truth. They think if they complain, others will have pity, but I think it's the other way around. Who can help you? A little pain — just take it and make yourself stronger. Take a deep breath. Try everything to heal yourself."

At eighty-nine when we met, she had cobbled together a life that was better than she could have imagined. She had a ridiculously cheap apartment in a ritzy part of town; a home attendant to do all the cooking, cleaning, and shopping, courtesy of Medicaid; food stamps and meals on wheels; and a daily mah-jongg game with fellow Cantonese speakers right in her building's activities room. For the first time in her life, she had ease and time to herself, with her needs met and no responsibilities toward others. She was never lonely because she always had friends around. Compared with the decades she spent working, raising a family, and nursing her dying husband, she had more financial security and fewer worries. "We're enjoying our life," she said. "Though we're not rich, we live a decent, better life. I can buy what I want, even expensive wool. Before, it was very difficult to get it."

The lessons of Ping began almost as soon as I met her. She seemed to be constantly translating them from one language to the other, pronouncing them one time in Cantonese, another time in English, teasing out different nuances in each. She viewed old age as a life stage like any other, in which "you must try to make yourself as happy as you can." Everyone will get old, she said. "It's a kind of experience. You have to keep yourself up all the time. Don't think of all those miserable things. Think all beautiful things, like when you were young, and how you enjoyed yourself, and like me, my husband, how good he was. I never think, oh, my husband died, I'm so sorry. No, never. I always think, he's always with me. That's why I'm keeping up myself."

Before I met Ping I spent weeks visiting Chinese and Korean senior centers, always with an interpreter, and meeting elders through social service agencies that catered to Latinos. Any portrait of old age in America, and especially in New York, would be incomplete without its immigrants, who bring a world of cultural values and practices to life's last stage. A few years ago, a group of elderly Korean gardeners in Queens feuded violently with city employees when the Parks Department tried to take control of their community garden, which their senior center had reclaimed from a trash-strewn lot. One gardener threatened to immolate himself with a can of gasoline and had to be talked down by the police department's hostage negotiation team. In another incident, police were called to remove a different group of older Koreans from a McDonald's because they spent whole days there, sometimes from early morning until after dark.

Cities like New York can be attractive places to get old, wherever you are from. Stores and doctors are within walking distance, and public transportation makes it possible to get around without a car. Whatever language you speak, you can find a community of others who do as well, including doctors and social workers. No one wants to be the only Fukienese speaker in an isolated retirement community in Arizona, or the only one talking Tagalog in a ballroom dancing class in Steamboat Springs.

As a result, the city has seen a boom of older immigrants, even as the number of native-born elders has declined. A 2013 study conducted by the Center for an Urban Future found that nearly half of New Yorkers ages sixty-five and up were foreign-born. Nationwide, the figure is closer to 11 percent, and has been dropping since 1960. Some, like Jonas Mekas, came as young people and assimilated smoothly into the city. Others, like the people I met at the Chinese or Korean senior centers, were more recent arrivals — often brought by their children to help raise the grandkids, now on their own without responsibilities or clearly defined purpose for their lives. They didn't circulate much outside their ethnic enclaves. Nearly a quarter of New York's foreign-born seniors live in poverty, and nearly two-thirds have limited proficiency in English. Only 8 percent of seniors from China — the second most common country of origin, after the Dominican Republic — speak English well, according to the report. These barriers make older immigrants less likely to access available support services and more likely to be isolated, lonely, and depressed.

At the sprawling Korean American Senior Center of Flushing, Queens, which serves 1,300 people on a typical day, a woman named Sun Kim, eighty-five, had some advice for me. "Don't stay home," she said. "Learn something." Her own education had been interrupted when her country was invaded by the north. When I asked her what young people should learn from their elders, she scoffed at the idea. "Your generation is better than my generation, so you have nothing to learn from me," she said. "You have more opportunities, so we can learn from your generation, because I didn't have the opportunity to learn because of the war. It's not a trauma. My daughters went to school and got educations, but I think I could have learned more."

I expected to find longing or nostalgia for the countries of their birth. American culture has a reputation for disregarding its elders. But I found the opposite. No one I met wanted to go back home, because life for elders was harder there, unless you were rich. So they jammed elbow to elbow at long, fluorescent-lit tables for hot meals and bingo, or read newspapers in their native language. Few spoke English. A woman named Qian Chin, who followed her daughter from Hong Kong in the 1960s, said she

187

didn't like the way America treated its elderly people, but then promptly reversed herself. "To be honest, the American government has done a better job than the Chinese government," she said. She received almost a thousand dollars a month in food stamps and Supplemental Security Income, and paid a little more than two hundred dollars a month for a subsidized apartment. "It's just kind of enough," she said, adding that her children gave her occasional pocket money. "Nine out of ten seniors I know have such benefits."

On a winter afternoon in her apartment, where she showed off her windows facing south — "It gets the most sunshine, and emperors always preferred facing south," she said — her grievance was not with the woes of old age, but with her daughter, who moved to North Carolina and never called. "She has luxury and time to travel, but can't make time to come here," Qian said. "I'm not asking too much, just a couple phone calls. She's not doing that. She's forgetting me as a daughter. Because she's been here too long, she adopted the American style."

Qian's son Henry, who was visiting from Connecticut, said that the difference between the United States and China was that in China, children were expected to take care of their elderly parents, but here, the government was expected to do it. He stuck up for his sister. "Mother's Day she calls," he said.

"Chinese New Year, birthday, and Christmas she'll call," Qian said. "Those are the countable occasions. I haven't seen her for three years. I'm not expecting her to visit all the time, just a day. Sometimes I miss her desperately and I cry alone."

Finally, she said, "I'm sad that my grandchildren don't speak Chinese at all. They were all born here. Maybe just a few words, like 'hello' or 'grandma.' So it's very difficult to communicate. I don't even have their phone numbers because of the language gap, and they're very busy."

Others I met at the senior centers were socially integrated or isolated, animated or sedentary, content or frustrated, ready to die or eager to carry on. When I met Ping Wong, she was all those things and more.

"I'm not lonely," Ping said the first time we met, embarking on a typical adventure in language, "because when I came here I got a job as an interpreter for a Filipino heart doctor. I worked there for eight years as a so-so interpreter. Here, there are thirty Chinese tenants in the building, and eighteen are Cantonese, so I help the boss with the China people. We play mah-jongg almost every day. So I still feel happy even though I live alone. Whenever there's a game, they say come."

As I got to know Ping, I began to recognize her narrative style. Most stories entailed a foray to some other part of her life, followed or preceded by a bit of advice for living, and always ending with mah-jongg. Several times I watched her play and was surprised to see that apart from explaining to me the rules of the game, the women played in near silence. "Mah-jongg," Ping explained over tiles one afternoon in the activities room, "is for playing, not for talking. We have no energy for anything but playing."

The drama of Ping's year involved her annual trip to Atlantic City with her daughter. In recent years, many of the casinos there had folded, but for Ping, the trips remained a highlight that she looked forward to. Then, in April, two weeks shy of her ninetieth birthday, she seemed to sink into unusually low spirits. Ping has a habit of laughing at unpredictable moments when she speaks English, probably to hide her discomfort with the language, but on this day she was clearly down: she had decided she was not well enough to go to Atlantic City. Three hours in a car was too long for her arthritic body. "Of course, I feel sorry for myself," she said, sounding defeated. "I don't want to be so old. You're growing stronger and stronger, and I'm getting weaker and weaker."

Her funk seemed to build around her as she talked, as if coming from some part of her that she rarely visited. "I tell you something funny," she said. "Sometimes I don't want to live too long. The pain is too much, and my bones hurt me terribly. So sometimes I want to die more than live. Ninety years old is long enough."

It was rare to see her like this, and it didn't last. The words seemed to make her self-conscious, and by the time I left, her conversational tone had returned to its normal hue. But I didn't know how much I should believe her.

These kinds of conversational reversals — celebrating her good fortune one minute, despairing the next — confused me at first, and made me think Ping's upbeat side might be an attempt to paint a happy image for her building or her peer group. After all, no one wants to be thought of as living in the slough of despond. Over time, though, I came to see Ping's contradictory views of her old age as an adaptive asset. Contentment for her wasn't unmediated joy, but came with a frank acknowledgment of the hardships in her life — the pain that would keep her from Atlantic City, the losses of her husband and son. Each of the elders had these mixed feelings to some degree, but with Ping, because of the language gap, they were especially pronounced.

Here, clearly, was a lesson about adversity, from someone who knew it intimately. Gerontologists consider the tendency to sustain mixed feelings, rather than try to resolve them, as a component of elder wisdom, a recognition that life doesn't have to be all good to be good, and also that it never will be. Troubles are always with us, and getting rid of this one or that won't make us happy; it'll just move another hardship to the head of the class. Karl Pillemer of Cornell makes the distinction between "happy in spite of" and "happy if only," the former being a benefit of old age, the latter a vexation of youth. "Happy in spite of" entails a choice to be happy; it acknowledges problems but doesn't put them in the way of contentment. "Happy if only" pins happiness on outside circumstances: if only I had more money, less pain, a nicer spouse or house, I'd be happy as a clam. "Happy if only" feeds millions of dollars into lotteries or impulse purchases, which provide nothing of the sort. Ping, by contrast, didn't expect her hardships to pass, so didn't pin her happiness on their doing so. When she was younger, she said, she thought moving to America would solve her problems; she found that it just replaced them with others. The lesson was to find happiness not in the absence of pain and loss, but in their acceptance.

As simple as this lesson sounds, I found it one of the most daunting to live by. Most accomplishments in my life, especially my professional life, have come from rejecting my dissatisfactions — not accepting adversity, but striving against it. Of course I never got clear of adversity, just found new faces for it, but the striving itself was a driving force. To spend time with Ping and the other elders was to reconsider these accomplishments and the efforts that went into them. At the end of eighty or ninety years, how much would they matter? In my year with the elders, none spoke of their professional accomplishments — a surprise, given how much of our lives we spend either working or obsessing about work. This was true even of Jonas Mekas, who was still creating significant work. The elders also never mentioned obstacles they had overcome. Somehow these things no longer seemed the measure of a life. Most were glad to retire, missing only the camaraderie of the workplace. They spoke instead of their families or close relationships, which they didn't measure as they would personal accomplishments — they wouldn't love their children more if they were more attentive or illustrious.

Researchers believe that each of us has a general "set point" or average level of happiness that we hover around through our lives' ups and downs. If something good happens — say, we win the lottery — we're joyful for a while, but eventually we return more or less to where we were before. Ditto with setbacks. This set point, which seems based on some combination of genes and environment, explains why some people can be happy in dire circumstances, and others miserable in enviable ones. But there is some evidence that we are not slaves to our set point — that we can nudge it upward by regular acts of gratitude or altruism, and by not brooding on our troubles. Ping kept her spirits up by accepting her pains as a part of life — not barriers to happiness but accompaniments to it. If she was going to have any contentment in her life, it was going to come with arthritis pain and her other losses. Happiness, she said, is when "you have a nice place to live in, and you have enough money to spend and a good family. That's it. And when you're young, you fulfill your dreams. I traveled. The world is so wonderful, so different. You should travel around the world and use up your money for sightseeing."

Ping was full of advice. See the world while you're young, she said. Make money. Spend money. Have fun. Don't indulge at the expense of your health or financial security. Be satisfied with your life. "Work is happiness, to make you live longer," she said one day. Often she talked about preparing for life's end, by which she meant financially, not philosophically. "The most important thing is money for your last day," she said. "One tenant here, a peasant from China, refuses to talk about her funeral. She says, 'If I die, let them throw me in the garbage. Why should I pay money for a funeral?'" Ping repeated this anecdote several times during the year, always with the same disapproval and pride that she had planned otherwise.

Like Sun Kim from the Korean senior center, Ping didn't believe that old age conferred wisdom. "Young people should be much better than the older," she said. "With science, every day things are changing. Now you can go to the moon. The elderly cannot think about it. There's no pleasure for the young people to absorb the older things. Older things, most of them have passed, because the world keeps going up."

On the other hand, she said, "When you're young, you don't know what you mean by happiness or sadness." Like the other elders, she had lost enough in her lifetime to know that even the worst losses were only devastating if she made them so. One day she mentioned a neighbor who had died recently, and another who had moved to a nursing home for dementia care. Both losses hurt her, she said, but the grief could also be therapeutic. "It takes your heart," she said. "But it can happen. Too smooth a life is not very good. You train your brain to deal with difficult challenges. When it passes, just let it go by. Next time, learn from it. I learn something from loss. If you never met something bad, you don't know how to deal with it when you do."

When I compared my life with Ping's, I was struck by how many "needs" I had that she managed to live without: professional

196

accomplishment, parental approval, my marriage, time at the gym, the right microgreens from the farmers market, an apartment that cost too much. Though I wouldn't want to give up all of these, spending time with Ping helped me see them as false needs, meaning huge sucks of time and energy that they only sometimes repaid. Even losing some of my mobility — my right foot was in a walking boot because of a torn plantar plate — didn't affect me in the ways I might have thought. My life was still my life, and I was still the one living it. A lesson of Ping was that I could hang on to these "needs," but I should value them for what they were worth, not as things I was afraid to lose. A different job, a different home, a little extra handle in my love handles wouldn't fundamentally change my life. They didn't matter as much as I thought they did.

One day in midyear, at a dim sum restaurant in Chinatown, I asked Ping what advice she would give her younger self. She had invited me along on an outing with her daughter, Elaine, who lived in New Jersey and was sixty-two at the time. Elaine said she often thought about her own old age when she was with her mother. "I look at her and think about how I'll look when I get old," she said. "I think I won't be as healthy as my mom. She looks healthier than I do. She exercises all the time, and I'm lazy." Ping's building offered regular exercise classes, and she had participated in past years, but by the time I met her, Ping, too, described herself as too lazy for exercise. In the last year, Elaine said she had noticed lapses in her mother's memory, coming more frequently lately. On this day, Ping seemed both tired and exhilarated from the effort of getting out, achy from the damp weather. She had been reading Sidney Sheldon novels recently, she said, which she liked because they immersed her in both the joys and the despairs of their characters.

"I would tell young people not to think about when you're older," she said, offering advice that seemed meant for her daughter as well as her younger self. "It's not good to think about old time, old time, old time. Old time of course is miserable. Or some part is good, some part is not good. How do you know? So I ask them not to think so far away. Think in front of you, how to keep yourself up, healthy, and make money, and how to spend money in the right way, not in the wrong way. Not necessary to think about old age. Keep yourself healthy and strong and make money." She laughed heartily, as if to dispel any aroma of self-pity. "The world is changing to the better," she said. "For my own life I'm getting better and better, too."

Luck helps. In 2005, Ping chanced across a notice in one of the Chinese-language newspapers for a new subsidized apartment building for seniors near Gramercy Park in Manhattan, with rents capped at 30 percent of residents' net income, after medical expenses. More than seven hundred people applied in the first wave, but Ping was one of the first selected; she even got a two-bedroom apartment and a fifty-dollar weekly stipend for helping the management work with the Chinese residents who didn't speak English. One of her new neighbors, in turn, told her where she could apply for a free home attendant. These benefits enabled her to be "independent," she said, meaning she didn't live with her daughter. After working and commuting until she was nearly eighty, she felt she was entitled to the government support now.

The building she found, Cabrini Apartments, came with an in-house social worker and occasional activities, and a building manager, Philip Deans, who made a point to get to know the residents. Informally, the residents helped one another tap available social services. Phil Deans, whom Ping called the "boss," said she was "about average" at navigating the city bureaucracy, including home care agencies, paratransit services, and food stamps. "She's aware of it but doesn't know how to tap into it," he said. But she was very outgoing, and sought out the building's social workers, he said.

Though she had medical problems, particularly joint pain, she tried to keep her mind on other things. "I never think of dying," she said one day. "Death is a very bad thing to think about. I lie in bed and I'm comfortable, but I say, move. I encourage myself to get up. It's not easy. But I need to move. It's good for the elderly to learn not to complain too much. People don't comfort you. You should comfort yourself."

She made choices. She didn't like to exercise, so she tended plants on her windowsill to keep her body active. When her Medicare Part D plan stopped covering lidocaine patches for her arthritis pain, she cut the patches she had in small pieces and supplemented them with Tylenol — enough relief to get her through her daily activities and mah-jongg games. Mah-jongg, too, forced her to move her arms and exercise her brain, and kept her in the social world where she thrived. Playing regularly, she said, kept her from getting bored or lonely. "It has so many benefits for your health," she said one day at the table, after winning a trick and asking the others to push the tiles her way because it hurt her to reach that far. "You use your mind. You use your body, even if it's just your hands." A good day, she said, was "when I play mah-jongg and win. I feel happy. We don't play for money, but winning makes my brain better."

When I asked Ping the secret to a long life, she said, "The first thing is you must make yourself happy. No one can say I haven't got bad times, hard times. Of course in a lifetime you have good times and bad times. When my son died, for two years I couldn't sleep well. Every night for two years. After that I adjusted myself, because I have a very good daughter here. I'm quite satisfied with my life here. I'm very lucky to live in this building."

This is what Ping taught me about thinking like an old person: try to be flexible, always recalibrating goals or what made a life worth living. A younger person might have camped out in her disappointment over canceling the trip to Atlantic City, wallowing in the sense that it made her special.

201

Instead, Ping released it. She knew how to give up things that once seemed important but no longer did, choosing happiness from among the stuff available to her.

This lesson made my life immensely easier. Attending to my false needs was a lot of work. Once I started letting them go, it freed me to focus on things that were more rewarding or lasting. It also meant I could stop feeling guilty about all the things I thought I should be doing but wasn't. Somebody else could practice daily mindfulness or find a shredder for my old bank statements. The right microgreens from the farmers market, it turned out, passed the test. They required minimal effort and enabled me to eat well. But other things in my life, not so much: half my clothes and other possessions, arguments at work or on social media, certain friends and family members who just brought me down — I let them go and didn't miss them.

Older people often confound younger people in what they consider important. In 1993 and 1994, researchers at four university medical centers asked hospitalized patients over age eighty whether they would rather live a year in their current state of health, or live a shorter period of time in excellent health. Then they asked the patients' health care surrogates — often their children — how they thought the patients would answer. It was a test of how older people, especially those with serious health problems, valued their remaining lives. To the surrogates, the question seemed obvious: of course a sick octogenarian would give up time in a hospital bed to live a healthier but shorter life. But the elders surprised them. Most said they would give up only one month or less to be in excellent health, and 40 percent said they were unwilling to give up any time. They chose time over health. When patients were interviewed again a year later, they were willing to give up even less time in exchange for excellent health, by an average of two weeks.

Even people with dementia, the biggest fear of many younger people, rate their quality of life much higher than their proxies do, according to a 2010 report by the British Mental Health Foundation, which surveyed forty-four people with dementia about their lives. The researchers expected that people would assess their quality of life in line with the state of their disease — the more their minds declined, the lower their quality of life. This was the view of the proxies, who were usually family caregivers. They saw Dad's quality of life as low and getting lower. But people with dementia saw their lives differently, and judged their quality of life by what they did — spend time with peers or family members, challenge themselves intellectually, enjoy nature — rather than by what they lost. They didn't think dementia was the most important thing about them.

As the researchers reported, "Dementia may not affect a person's quality of life in respect of emotions, feelings and mental well-being in ways that one would expect." Even as the disease advanced, paring away more of their memories and cognitive powers, their assessment of their quality of life remained unchanged. The researchers called this both "counter-intuitive" and an "important finding, not least because of the increased use of living wills where people effectively make predictions concerning how they may feel in the future about living with certain types of conditions." What's clear is that dementia lessens the quality of life for many patients' caregivers, and that these are the people whose voices we most often hear on the ravages of Alzheimer's and other dementias.

By her birthday in May, Ping felt well enough to go to a buffet lunch and then dinner with her daughter. Then, at the end of the summer, she received a welcome surprise: her daughter-in-law and grandson were visiting from China, and planned to go to Atlantic City. And they were bringing a great-grandson she had never met. This made Ping reconsider her pains. Were they completely unmanageable? Or were they something she could tolerate for the pleasures of seeing her family? What was important to her? The three-hour drive no longer seemed the biggest thing in her life. She decided to go to Atlantic City after all, despite the pain she knew she would suffer. It was the best decision of her summer, she said afterward. "When you're very happy, you forget everything," she said. "We talked the whole way. So I forgot the pain in my body."

Over the year, though, some changes in Ping were noticeable. Her conversation became choppier, and she had trouble maintaining a train of thought. Then, in February 2016, a troubling sign. She called asking to talk to me about something very important; it couldn't wait. But when I got to her apartment she could not remember why she had called. She laughed at her confusion. "Getting old," she said. "Not easy to remember." But the lapse clearly troubled her. This was a new development, one that was always a possibility with any of the six elders in this project. She stood slowly and looked around the room, as if surprised by her lost train of thought. Where had it gone? Yet she was still so unmistakably Ping, constructing herself from bits and pieces of a long life. She'd seen friends recede into dementia. Now one of her pieces was missing. She laughed to cover her embarrassment. Did it mean she will forget more tomorrow? Or was it just another loss in a life that had seen many and always kept going? Finally she remembered — she wanted me to complain to the building manager about her new linoleum. Here were the conflicting forces of old age, toward order and decay: Ping's drive to keep shaping her world against her memory's slide toward disorder.

The next time I visited, a few months later, there was no sign of this confusion. So it is with memory and old age. Good days and bad days, neither a guarantee of what tomorrow will bring. She talked lucidly about her life under Mao, when she needed ration tickets to buy rice, and about her first years in her building. She had another birthday coming up already, maybe another trip to Atlantic City — she wasn't sure. As on previous visits, she showed off souvenirs from her European travels, including a wineglass from the Czech Republic, reminders of who she was, a traveler, even if she rarely left the building.

When her home attendant brought out a photo of Ping as a young woman, Ping laughed. "She wants to show you how beautiful I was," she said, stopping to laugh some more. "It's the past. Old lady already."

Yet she was still working to make things better for herself. She asked for help with her English. It wasn't too late to learn more, she said. "Suppose you and me are good friends for years," she asked. "Can we say 'I miss you'?"

The new linoleum on the floor now pleased her, especially compared with the moldy carpet it replaced. Wasn't it a big improvement, she said, another reason she was blessed to live in her apartment — another reason to be happy? She was doing what she always did, rescaling her expectations to the world as it came at her, rather than fighting against it. This was her way of choosing happiness. Even her disruption offered one more reason to celebrate.

"It's clean and better for my health," she said of the linoleum. And she laughed again. "Maybe I live longer and you have to come more." The laughter cascaded down and didn't stop. It would be the last time I heard her laugh like that.

NINE:
THE LESSONS OF JOHN

"I'M NOT SAD ABOUT ANYTHING,
BUT I'VE HAD ENOUGH."

As a matter of fact, I hope there isn't an afterlife. I can't imagine anything going on forever. I miss Walter and I wish I could meet him in another life, but I know I won't. Actually it's rather soothing. It is all going to end; I don't see anything wrong with that.

— John Sorensen, ninety-one

John Sorensen taught the most difficult lesson of all: how to accept death and still go on living. He wasn't depressed and he wasn't really suicidal — not actively so, though he sometimes said he wished he were. Often he was happy. He relished the memories of his life, from his boyhood in upstate New York to his long love affair with Walter Caron. He lived in an apartment he had decorated exactly as he wanted it, which was important to him. He just wanted to die. "I've had a wonderful life," he said. "I was sorry at first I didn't have a bigger career, but Walter was more than a substitute for that. We had a very good life." But after ninety-one years, he said, "Life doesn't have enough compensation for me now. I'll be glad to go."

By the time I met John in the beginning of 2015, I knew how to kill a person without causing pain or suffering. I won't share the method here, but the Internet is full of such helpful information. A few years before, I had looked into the possibility of killing my mother. This was after her second spinal fusion operation — after the infection that almost killed her, after she blamed my brother and me for authorizing the feeding tube that enabled her to survive. I was back from Iraq, resettled into my marriage and life in New York. Since the surgery, my mother had fallen and suffered a compression fracture to the vertebra just above the operation. The bone, which had become porous over the years, collapsed like a brittle sponge, the doctor explained. There was no treatment to make it structurally sound again.

The pain in the coming months was more than my mother could bear. It absorbed her life. Her pain was a sea and she was swimming in it, with no shore in sight, and she didn't want to see one. She hated physical therapy, which involved intentionally moving in ways that hurt, and she was getting diminishing relief from her painkillers. A pain management specialist recommended electronically deadening some of the nerves around her spine, which provided some relief and raised her spirits. But the pain came back at least as strong as before, and now there were zero magic bullets to give her hope. One day she collapsed in bed with her head at the foot end, and there she stayed, moaning when her aides changed the absorbent pad underneath her.

That was when I started gathering information on assisted suicide. I owed her that much, I thought.

It never came to that, fortunately. The doctor in her building upped her painkillers until she was finally able to move around, and she gradually returned to her old life: eating dinner with the same friends, going on occasional outings in the building's van, taking weekly classes in Spanish and ceramics. Thanks to her motorized scooter, she was as mobile as she needed to be. Her aides provided companionship and comfort. The problem was that she still wanted to die. "I was very bitter," she told me later. "I lost my faith in God. I didn't think God would love me and want me to live on in this way. I still think that in a way." I could see the justness in quitting a life reduced to writhing on a soiled absorbent pad. But wasn't it indulgent to want release from a life with so many hard-earned comforts?

She didn't think so. Instead she quoted an old verse, which she attributed to James Joyce: " 'Tis old I am and tired I am, and I want to go down the river to the sea," she said. Her productive years were behind her, she said, and all she saw in front of her was more pain and decline. "That's the way I look at it. Maybe at the moment I might be afraid, I don't know. And it's a rightful thing. You wouldn't want to hang on too long."

I rarely visited John without thinking of my mother. A paradox of John was that he loved to talk, so that even talking about his desire to die cheered him up. As a kid he'd regularly gotten into trouble for talking too much, and as an old man he liked to repeat this story, usually after a good, rambling conversation in which he did most of the talking. Even when he talked about death he'd smile and grow animated and soon move on to other topics. Unlike my mother, he seemed to savor the pleasures that were still available to him. One day I visited after he had heard the soprano Sondra Radvanovsky in Verdi's *A Masked Ball* on the Metropolitan Opera radio broadcast, and his whole face lit up to talk about it. "I think I was up in the air for several days after that," he said. "I hadn't heard singing like that in a long, long time. It makes me feel very much alive. When she finished I was on a high for a week."

He seemed astonished that the world still produced such beauty — a new divine soprano — even though he no longer did. Music took away all other context. Just days before, he had heard Glenn Miller's "A String of Pearls" on the radio and suddenly been moved to dance all alone in the kitchen. "I finally got up and held on to the refrigerator and tried to dance to that," he said. "It was wonderful. Music makes me excited and it makes me happy."

When I first started visiting John, whenever he talked about wanting to die I'd point out all these things that gave him pleasure, citing them as reasons to carry on. Didn't he want to hear Jonas Kaufmann one more time, or see his friends Mike and John from Fire Island? Why this day and not three days from now or three years? This was an automatic reflex on my part, the kind we offer friends when they're feeling low: cheer up, at least you're not digging up stumps in

213

the hot sun. I'd remind him of friends who wanted him to live, as if the problem were that he didn't know he was loved. I was echoing the parts of our culture that glorify battlers: no surrender, don't be a quitter, fight to the finish. Quitting seemed somehow weak or misguided — or, in the celestial good vibes of Deepak Chopra, a failure of imagination, because any of us can become "pioneers in a land where . . . old age, senility, infirmity, and death do not exist and are not even entertained as a possibility." Death may be the one thing guaranteed to all of us, but it is also one of the few things it is still shameful to want.

But John never wavered. His desire to die wasn't blind or headstrong. He was more like a singer who had finished his song and didn't have another verse to perform. Why stay on the stage, huffing and sweating under the floodlights, with nothing left to give or gain? The frailties of old age were getting bigger and he was getting smaller, and the most he could expect in return for fighting them would be the chance to do so again the next day, when he was even more bruised and sore. The resizing was literal — John had been six feet tall but was only five feet eight the last time he was measured, and he figured he had shrunk since then.

"I'm ready to go right now," he said. "Give me a day or two." Maybe he was going to die in two weeks, maybe in 3.7 years, the average life expectancy for an American man at age ninety-one; either way, the remaining time meant nothing to him. To friends he'd already given whatever he had to give, and from them received whatever he could hold.

What I came to realize with John was that accepting death — wishing for it, even — didn't devalue the days he had left, but made each count more because they were so few. It freed him to live in the things he liked, not agonizing over what he would do if he could. This was why talking about wanting to die could cheer him up. Death gave everything its value. The number of times he would see this or that friend was limited, so each time was precious. The moments were supersaturated, not fleeting as they are in youth. Watching an old movie reminded him of his parents or Walter or his jones for Dana Andrews or a party on Fire Island. Or all of these things at once. Since he didn't believe in an afterlife, death was an ending for him, not a transition or destination, so he didn't think about it except as an inevitability, without shape or color. It was no reason to look past the present moment. He didn't hope for more, and he didn't want to hope for more. Such hope made no sense to him; it was an appetite that he had left behind.

The psychologist Mary Pipher, in her compassionate book *Another Country: Navigating the Emotional Terrain of Our Elders,* writes that in old age people "look for their existential place. They ask, 'How did my life matter?' 'Was my time well spent?' 'What did I mean to others?' 'What can I look back on with pride?' 'Did I love the right people?' And they search for a home and a village where they will be comfortable, useful, and loved." As far as I could tell, John didn't do any of this, at least by the time I met him. He had moved past the questioning stage, because the answers no longer meant anything to him. He knew what he enjoyed and what mattered to him, what he had lost and could never regain. It drove him mad to feel no longer useful, and he took only limited comfort from knowing that he was loved. If he had earlier looked for his existential place or searched for a home, such strivings had passed. Instead he made peace with the things he had given up. "I always planned in my old age to read and play the piano, and I can't do either one," he said. "Do you know what you want to do when you get old?"

Each time I visited he led me through pleasant memories, sometimes the same ones again and again. His life was a small jewel box, but a brightly shining one. He talked about his love of furniture as a child, about hearing the soprano Kirsten Flagstad on the radio in 1935, when he was twelve, and discovering a whole world outside his small upstate New York town. His favorite operas were Wagner, of course. "I wish you could have known my mother when she was young," he said one day, and that was all he needed to set off on a journey. Boredom, fear, anger, jealousy, hurt, betrayal, loneliness — all were absent from his memories. Instead there was love and sex and warmth, time with friends and a beach house he built with Walter. What had seemed a morbid fixation on death was also a shortcut to enjoying whatever time lay in front of him. Since death was part of the immutable sequence of things, accepting it gave his life more order. Anything else was unbalanced, like a chord that doesn't resolve or an unmade bed. It comforted John to imagine the last piece falling into place, symmetry and order and wholeness at last.

"Do you remember the war?" John asked me one day in April. "It's very hard for me to think about adults not remembering the war or the Depression. To me it is only like yesterday. None of my friends remember it, the Second World War. I remember when Pearl Harbor was attacked; I was pressing a pair of pants for school the next day. And none of us knew where Pearl Harbor was. We knew we'd been attacked somewhere, but we didn't know where Pearl Harbor was. I was at home. I was very fussy about my clothes then."

We were sitting, as we always did, in his two favorite chairs, low-set Louis XVI armchairs that John had upholstered himself, now frayed because his hands were too stiff to mend them. They were terribly uncomfortable, especially for John, who had trouble lowering himself into them and raising himself out, but he refused to trade them for something more practical. You never got too old to care about appearances, he said. The day before, he had tried to walk to the corner with his aide, but had lost his strength and gotten scared after just a few steps, and had to be helped home, both legs throbbing in pain. "He wanted to pick me up and carry me, but I wouldn't let him," John said of his aide. "I'm not ready to give up to that point yet. I hate giving up things, I guess." He looked at me and said, "You know, I can't see you yet. I see a shadow, that's all I see." It was nearly the last time John left his apartment except to go to the doctor and then, finally, the hospital.

My year with John sometimes felt like an idiosyncratic tour of the previous American century. He missed the war because of an irregular heartbeat, but lived through the Depression, Truman (he was con), Nixon (he was pro), the sexual revolution (he was promiscuous), and the advent of a gay rights movement. He hated Elvis until he saw him in *Loving You,* at which point he fell in love. When patrons at the Stonewall Inn rebelled against a police raid in 1969, John said the consensus in Fire Island was that the revolt would just make things worse. Always it amazed him that gay people could marry. He and Walter had registered as domestic partners and kept a certificate in the bathroom, alongside a yellowing 1990 article about Walter closing the bookstore that he ran, Isaac Mendoza, the city's oldest. They were old men who had gotten old together, two accomplishments for gay men of their generation. By the time Walter went to the doctor in Fire Island with what he thought was constipation in 2009, he had already lived eight years longer than anyone in his family.

"He was the happy one," Anne Kornblum, Walter's niece, said of her uncle, sitting with John in his apartment. "You were the dour one."

"He was no happier than I was," John said. "We were both happy."

Walter died at home on October 11, 2009, after stints in the hospital and rehab. By the end, he had stopped closing his eyes, even when he slept, so it was hard to tell when he was conscious, and his breathing was so shallow it was almost imperceptible. John didn't seem saddened talking about that night, perhaps because it was safely in the past, or because it was a time he felt very close to Walter. "I went in one time and said, 'I don't know,' " he said. "I couldn't tell. I left and came back a little while later and it was obvious. That was a tough night. I called 911. The police came. I was a wreck. I'll never forget how nice the police were. It took a lot of calls to get a doctor to confirm a natural death. It took at least three hours before the undertaker could come for him. The police wouldn't release him before we got the okay."

If they had married, John would have been eligible to receive Social Security survivor benefits of about three thousand dollars a month. But New York did not recognize same-sex marriage until after Walter died; John's Social Security and a small pension came to about half that — barely enough to cover the rent, let alone living expenses. That was when Anne took a new role in John's life.

Anne, who was sixty-one when I met her, was a force of nature, and the only woman I've ever watched answer an e-mail about what kind of holster she wanted. Besides caring for John, she worked full-time as a criminal investigator for the U.S. Postal Service and managed the care of her mother and both of her husband's parents. Her father-in-law was ninety-six and had severe dementia; her mother-in-law, who cared for him, was almost ninety. Her mother, who was in an assisted living facility in Massachusetts, "is in the worst shape of them all," she said. When anything went wrong, Anne got the call. If you have an Anne Kornblum in your life, consider yourself lucky. If not, you might want to find one.

To Anne, Uncle Walter and Johnny were the dashing couple who lived in New York

City and knew all about theater and music. John had exquisite taste and could fix anything. "Up until five years ago he was doing a hundred push-ups every day," she said.

John almost laughed. "I couldn't do it today because I'd never get up off the floor," he said. Being around Anne aroused his sense of humor. She let him say a woman couldn't be president, even though she didn't like it.

"You came out to Fire Island in winter, when there was no running water," he said. "We all had jugs and we went down to the town pump. No heat, kerosene lanterns. At Thanksgiving we all sat in coats and gloves. We had a helluva good time."

"I think alcohol had a lot to do with it," she said.

He couldn't believe the good fortune they had shared.

In short order, Anne took control of John's finances, applied for a senior citizen's rent freeze, moved his banking to a branch near his apartment, organized his medical care, got him a home attendant and two volunteer visitors from different agencies, and applied for Medicaid. When his doctor ordered a hundred days of full-time aides after a hospital stay, John wouldn't let them touch anything in the apartment, so they just sat around with this man who didn't want them there. But this didn't discourage Anne. By the time I met her, she was ready — and she thought John was ready — to apply for another round.

"John is actually in the best shape of my four old people," she said in August, at John's apartment. "But he's the most difficult. But it is what it is. It's all a negotiation. It's a gift to have them at this stage of life. But it's challenging. It gets stressful."

Despite Anne's presence, it was a bad day for John. When I arrived at his apartment he had a bright red bruise spreading over his upper arm and a blood-smeared bandage around one shin. There was a streak of blood on one of the kitchen cabinets. He wavered unsteadily on his feet. He couldn't remember how he fell.

"I could've fallen twenty or thirty times today, but I caught myself," he said, his voice quavering just above a whisper. Anne guided him to a favorite chair.

"That's why you need to use your walker," she said. "On days like that, get it out, use it."

"I use the cane," he said.

"Cane's not going to stop you from falling. A cane just makes you a tripod."

"I hate the looks of a walker. If you put the walker anyplace in this room it'd drive me crazy. I couldn't stand it. It'd be so ugly."

And so on. They both knew their lines, but still Anne pressed.

"I tell him, if he falls and breaks something, his life is going to change drastically. And it will bring into question whether he can stay here. Because once he goes into the hospital with something broken, it's sort of out of my hands what happens to him."

Anne examined John's arms and legs for other bruises. She did not say what they both knew: that she was doing all she could to keep him alive and out of a nursing home, and that no matter how much effort she put in, at some point it was a battle she would lose.

The story of America's aging population is to a great extent the story of people like Anne, the friends or family members who provide informal care, usually without training, and at great expense in time and money. Unpaid caregivers provide 90 percent of long-term care for the old or disabled, with most of them juggling caregiving along with jobs, families, and other responsibilities. A 2014 study by the RAND Corporation estimated that Americans spend thirty billion hours annually caring for older relatives and friends, at a cost in lost wages or time of $522 billion. The National Institutes of Health warn that caregiving "creates physical and psychological strain over extended periods of time, is accompanied by high levels of unpredictability and uncontrollability, has the capacity to create secondary stress in multiple life domains such as work and family relationships, and frequently requires high levels of vigilance. Caregiving fits the formula for chronic stress so well that it is used as a model for studying the health effects of chronic stress." But the report noted that providing care can also have positive benefits for the caregiver, and that "supporting or helping others may be just as beneficial to health as receiving support."

John's fall and the events leading up to it show how tenuous the networks of care can be.

John relied on regular visits from Anne and weekly visits from his home attendant and two friendly visitors. Anne coordinated the help and managed John's finances; the three visitors kept him company and ran errands, including refilling his prescriptions. I always scheduled my visits around them, because John didn't want anything to interfere with his time with Alex, Markus, and Scott.

In early August, Anne's mother-in-law fell and had to be hospitalized for a week, which left her father-in-law, who has severe dementia, in their apartment alone. Anne and her husband alternated twelve-hour shifts with him, but since Anne doesn't drive, she didn't leave even when her husband was on duty. This was a mistake, she realized. "I should have taken a walk around the building," she said. "You learn as you go along."

While she was busy with her father-in-law, one of John's volunteer caregivers missed a weekly session to go to a wedding, and another left for a brief vacation. By the time his home attendant's rotation came around, John had run out of his supply of trazodone, an antidepressant that he took to help him sleep. The drugstore had none on hand and had to order more.

John grew agitated from so much time alone and didn't sleep well without his meds. When he finally fell in his kitchen, it was from exhaustion as much as anything. Anne arrived at his apartment to find him bloody, bruised, and lonely. She, too, was worn out from her weeklong stay with her father-in-law.

She filled John's prescription and brought

him pizza from an old favorite restaurant; she cleaned the blood from his leg and from a kitchen cabinet; she helped him walk to the bathroom, saying, "I don't need any more accidents." She surveyed the house for hazards. "My concern is his medication, because I come in and find pills on the floor all over the place. He can't see them. He drops them. The heart pill is the most important for him to take regularly, and if he can't remember if he took it or not, not to take another one. Because he told the doctor if he can't remember he just takes another one."

Anne shrugged. Her mother-in-law was back home, but her mother was in a hospital in Massachusetts after eating tomatoes, which always irritate her colitis.

"She says, 'I like tomatoes,' " Anne said. Her mother also liked the attention from doctors, so going to the hospital was a social outing, Anne said. "It gets" — she searched for the right word — "challenging," she said, and sighed.

Soon there would be more crises, involving three of her four elders.

John was eighty-six and healthy for the first year after Walter died, maintaining the beach house and the apartment, even using a chain saw in the yard. Then, shortly after Labor Day in 2010, things took a turn. He knelt down to pick up something from the floor of his apartment and suddenly couldn't get up. He hadn't been feeling ill, but he just kept sliding lower until he was on his stomach. "At first I felt, this is silly," he said. "I just couldn't get up. Finally I got scared." He remembered somehow getting into an ambulance, telling the paramedics not to fuss with him, to let him die. The culprit, it turned out, was probably West Nile virus, which overruns the slower immune systems of older people. John was in and out of consciousness for three weeks, and in rehab until nearly Thanksgiving. By the time he got back home his muscles were weak from disuse, and by 2014, the year before I met him, he stopped going to Fire Island altogether. Complications with his digestion made it uncomfortable to go to the opera or theater, so he stopped that as well. He still had friends who visited him in New York, but his world was smaller, and the things that gave him the most new pleasure were slipping further away.

John's goal for the year I visited him was to spend Thanksgiving with friends outside the city, but as early as March he said he didn't think he would be well enough to go.

He didn't want to embarrass himself by his messy eating habits or the open revolt that was his daily digestion. John had gladly excused Walter's infirmities as products of disease and aging, not personal failings. But he rarely afforded himself the same slack. His friends' house had a gravel walk and stairs that he dreaded. He couldn't even dress himself the way he wanted, which remained important to him. For the next seven months, he remained pessimistic about attending. Still, he said, "That's the only thing I really look forward to."

By November, John felt well enough to go, even managed to use a knife and fork at the table. His closest friends were there, all twenty years his junior because everyone his age was dead. A month later, they all gathered at a restaurant near John's apartment for his ninety-second birthday, an event he'd hoped never to see. Anne's grandson was there, meaning four generations under one roof. For all the catastrophic talk, there had been no major health crises in his year, just a slow deterioration of his muscles and organs, more gaps in his short-term memory, more sleep problems, less mobility.

Was he living long or dying long? My mother wanted release from ever-insistent pain; John, by contrast, felt too much blankness, and didn't see the point in continuing. Why watch his favorite movie one more time when he already knew all the words and could no longer see the pictures? Each viewing could only offer less than the one before.

What he looked forward to now, he said, was having his ashes spread with Walter's on Fire Island. He had performed the duty for friends who passed before him, and he was sure his friends would do the same for him.

"That'll be a good day for me," he said, his tone casual. "It really will. I have a very few very good friends who will be sad. But I think they'll also know that's what I wanted, so it won't be too bad. It doesn't scare me at all. The other night I went through something where I thought, Jesus, there's some strange thing going on with my body, maybe I'm dying now. And I wasn't the least bit worried."

What could younger people learn from someone like John, who insisted he had no lessons to impart? The simplest answers were compassion and empathy; time with John was always time well spent because it was time inside the life of another person. There was courage in letting others see what it was like to get old, and kindness in sharing his dependency with Anne, even as he disliked being dependent. On one of my last visits, I asked what I should say to my mother the next time she said she wanted to die.

It puzzled him to think about this. It meant thinking forward, into a life other than his, which he didn't do. He knew that the things people said to him — "They say they don't want me to go yet" — didn't change anything, but reminded him of their friendship and their better times together. "Does she remember most of her life?" he said. "Did she have a nice life?"

Part of John's good life, I think, lay in his ability to fashion his memories into a story of a good life. John never saw a paradox in loving his life and also wanting to leave it. What a pain it must be to have other people — younger people, who could not know what it was to be old — presume to judge whether you had earned the right to die. What kind of society does that to people? What kind of friends? What kind of son? Maybe the best response to my mother's wish to die was just to tell her that I love her and will continue to do so. I'm working on that, too.

After that visit, Anne told me that John

didn't remember who had come to see him. He knew it was someone with a recorder, but couldn't say whether it was me. In a sense, I thought, I really hadn't been there with him, not in the same way as the people from his past who filled his conversation. I wasn't there in the way that Walter was there. That was only right, I thought, though sticklers might disagree. In one of our last conversations, John told a story about breaking his leg and getting out of gym class, then going to a dance and jitterbugging right in front of the gym teacher. The story still cracked him up. Of course he didn't remember me. He was going to die soon and he knew it, and he had so many other things to remember, eighty-six good years' worth to cram into whatever brief time was left to him.

At our first meeting, back in early 2015, I'd thought he was one of the most morbid people I'd ever met. But I was mistaken. The lesson of John Sorensen was that to accept death was to accept life, and to accept life was to live in joy, however dire the circumstances around you.

TEN:
THE LESSONS OF HELEN

"I WAS YOUR AGE; YOU WERE NEVER MY AGE."

I used to feel sorry for people who went to nursing homes. My father used to say that's where they beat you up. Nobody beats up anybody here. He didn't even know us at the end.

— Helen Moses, ninety-one

Helen Moses has a gentle way about her, and if you don't believe it just ask her. For instance, one day she told me about making new friends in her nursing home. "Like that girl that I called fat," she said. "She's my best friend now. She was very hot, and I didn't mean to be mean. I said, 'Fat people are usually very warm.' So she called me an asshole. So the next time I saw her she gave me a dirty look, and I said, 'Well, you're still fat.' Now she likes me, now that she got to know me. She told me her daughter is getting married next November. I wished her a lot of luck. But she's still fat."

The lessons of Helen, you may be surprised to learn, involve diplomacy and personal relationships.

It was a May afternoon, and Helen said she had been up all night because the Mets lost. The neon sign by her bed, which she lit whenever the team won, hung forlorn and dark behind her. She was talking about this and that, including the nurses who chase Howie out of her room at night, when suddenly she dropped a bombshell.

"I want to get married," she said. "Maybe we will in the summer."

I was visiting with two colleagues, a photographer and videographer, and it's possible that she wanted to make an impression, but the words were clear, and she seemed to have given them some thought. At her age, she said, "What's the point in hanging around together?"

She wouldn't wear a wedding dress, she said, because she had worn one for her first wedding, even though she and Howie were devotees of the cable show *Say Yes to the Dress,* about the search for the perfect wedding dress. Howie sat in his wheelchair by her bed, reaching a hand for hers. Asked how he felt about getting married, he appeared surprised by the question. "I feel fine about it," he said. When he'd had a moment to think, he was more effusive.

"It's like perfect heaven," he said. "It really is. Nothing but heaven. She's so perfect for me."

"What a lie," Helen said.

Howie looked offended. "Why?" he said.

"What about Theresa?" Helen said. Theresa was Theresa Caputo, a psychic on the TLC network, known as the Long Island Medium. Her hair is very big and very blonde. Howie went back to being quiet.

Plus, Helen said, there was a woman in their copper enameling class who tried to make out with Howie. She shot him a look. I couldn't tell whether he noticed. Probably they played this scene from time to time; their relationship, like many, seemed built on familiar set pieces, the way more long-standing relationships are built on shared memories.

Was she jealous? I asked.

"Nah," she said. "I can get whoever I want."

But the bravado was fleeting. Helen confessed that she had not told her daughter, Zoe, about wanting to get married. "I'm so nervous that I scratched myself and I'm bleeding," she said. Then she gathered herself. "It doesn't matter," she said, "because I'm going to do what I want to do."

My year with Helen now had an arc: a

planned wedding, a clash with Zoe, a reso-
lution of some sort. Something had to give,
and soon. But as the months went by, it
didn't. Helen said there wasn't going to be
a wedding; then she said maybe there
would. Then it was off again, then maybe
on. The couple still watched *Say Yes to the
Dress* every Sunday, and Zoe visited every
week, but nothing moved in either direction. Every time I asked Helen the status
she gave a different answer.

It took me a year to see how much elder
wisdom went into this suspended state.
Here was the shortened perspective of old
age at work: with a limited time frame in
front of her, she didn't need to start a new
life together with Howie, especially if it
would cause problems with Zoe. She needed
more of what she had now, even if it meant
leaving the conflict unresolved. A younger
woman with a long future in front of her
might place progress above all else, trusting
that change would be for the better. For
Helen, though, stasis brought extra attention and care. Postponing the battle for
another day kept the passions high without
burning any bridges. Maybe this wasn't
genius, but any of us who has fought battles
that aren't worth fighting can recognize its
wisdom. Helen, for all her impetuousness,

saw things for what they were. Losing Howie or Zoe, even for a minute, wasn't worth what she had to gain. She put the people in her life ahead of abstract principle.

Her lesson was the subtlest of all those I learned over the year. She had two people who loved her, each in a different way. Her wisdom was to figure out what they wanted to give her, and to create the circumstances that enabled each to give it.

Did she think she was wise? I asked.

She smiled at the question. "No one ever called me that," she said.

When I first started to seek out older people, I was particularly eager to meet someone who had found new love in old age. What was love like in one's eighties or nineties — not the love within a long-lasting marriage, which is anchored in shared experience, but love that both partners enter into knowing it cannot last too long? How do people that age begin to open up to someone new? At the Hebrew Home at Riverdale, new couples were hard to find, for a simple reason: the average stay at the home was about two years, and the end was rarely a condo on the beach. Helen and Howie were the exception, and she flaunted it. "I'm always happy," she said, and then gave her definition of happiness: "Not to think of any bad things. To let everything go. But young people are too young to understand."

The Hebrew Home, which began in a small Harlem synagogue in 1917 as a refuge for poor elderly immigrants, is a sprawling, comfortable place on the sloped bank of the Hudson River, with signs for the extensive fund-raising campaigns that enable it to provide care beyond that paid for by Medicaid. Whenever Helen and Howie discussed marriage, she always said she didn't want to leave the home, even though she hated the food. "I'm not leaving this room," she said one day after glee club, where the couple joined a dozen or so others in recording songs for a CD, to be distributed to residents and their families. "Howie, will you join me? You promised, remember?" Other times, though, she complained about the other residents or the fact of being in an institution.

"Sometimes I want to go home," she said. "But I can't. There's no place I can go."

Nursing facilities like the Hebrew Home are a relatively recent invention. Until the nineteenth century, almost all medical care, including care for elders, took place in the home. Old people without family support went to crude public almshouses, which provided a roof and minimal sustenance for orphans, people with mental illnesses, alcoholics, widows, and people who were too poor or frail to care for themselves. The institutions were meant to shelter the public from the corruptions of the poor as much as the other way around. In the twentieth century, as medicine and social programs advanced, children moved out of the almshouses to orphanages, the mentally ill to asylums or sanitariums, and the treatably ill to hospitals, leaving the almshouses as places of last resort for destitute elders and people with severe disabilities. The Social Security Act, passed in 1935, provided an income that enabled reasonably healthy old people to leave the almshouses and live on their own. For the remaining old and disabled residents, now enriched with government checks to pay for care, there formed privately operated "rest homes" and "convalescent homes," pleasantly named precursors to the modern nursing home. In 1954, there were more than a quarter million nursing home beds in America, and by 1965, the year Lyndon Johnson signed Medicare into effect, nearly a half million. By December 31, 2014, there were 1.4 million Americans living in nursing homes, though the numbers had been dropping slightly for a decade. For some, the institutions provided independence from their children.

The new homes belonged to a class of institutions, like orphanages and prisons, where people went about all their activities under one roof, among others more or less like themselves, and according to rules dictated by central authorities. Segregation by age and physical capacity became goals rather than ills. The priorities of nursing homes — to keep the frailest residents alive and healthy and keep costs down — were not always those of the individuals living there. Safety and efficiency trumped other concerns. You couldn't have a cocktail lounge or an unregulated front door, for example, because it wouldn't be safe, even though many residents might want to drink or come and go without telling anyone. You couldn't have breakfast at 4:00 p.m. because the staff couldn't manage it.

At the nursing home, Zoe made sure Helen never felt abandoned, calling her several times a day and visiting once or twice a week, often spending time with Helen's neighbors on the floor. The visits were a point of pride for Helen. Other residents often went long stretches without anyone coming to see them. She had a mate and a daughter, both devoted to her. "I feel sorry for old people who live by themselves and have nobody to come help them or come make them feel happy for a couple hours," she said. "Everybody should have a daughter like Zoe." Helen's periodic feuds with other residents, similarly, meant that she was never forgotten by the staff. Helen liked to cut a big figure. "If you don't see me, you hear me," she said often.

For Helen's first four months in the nursing home, Zoe was used to having her mother to herself on visits. Then suddenly Howie was there, and wouldn't leave the two alone. Often he sidetracked conversations with comments that took a long time to finish. His disability, which meant he needed an attendant to wheel him anywhere, also seemed to Zoe to limit her mother's activities. It was typical of Helen to put Howie's needs ahead of her own, Zoe said. But what about Zoe's needs? "I want to savor every minute I have with my mother," she said. "Is that such a crime? Other people have my mother seven days a week. When I come, I'm very protective of who comes near my mother. If you want to call that selfish, I'm selfish. I want my time with my mother. There's things that I need to share with my mother that nobody else

241

needs to know."

It was a cool spring afternoon, and Howie was at the weekly copper enameling class, which gave Zoe time alone with her mother. Around them were photographs of mother and daughter at various ages, along with pictures of other relatives and the neon Mets logo. When Helen moved to the home from her house upstate, Zoe helped her pare her possessions to these few. "This is who my mother is," Zoe said: "her pictures, her family, her grandchildren, history with my dad, pictures of my dad." She did not mention Howie. In Zoe I could see the domineering force that Helen had once been. "She looks like me but she's prettier," Helen said.

When Helen moved to a different floor, Zoe saw to it that Howie moved as well. If Helen fell or got a cold, Zoe pressed the home for treatment, and she interceded in her mother's disputes with other residents. When Helen thought a man had pushed her over in an argument about a newspaper, Zoe told her to let it go.

"You know what?" Zoe said. "Both of you were wrong."

"This time I wasn't wrong," Helen said.

"That's fine," Zoe said. "But you need to move on and be a mensch."

For Helen, who was used to living and working around people younger than she, going into the Hebrew Home was a sudden immersion in the world of her peers, including many with dementia. She didn't mind the regimented schedule, but she often complained about the other residents. "I hate some of them here," she said. "Some of them don't have their marbles and there's no one to talk to that has any education."

This, I came to see, was the blustery Helen. Another side of her socialized widely and joined in group activities. She sang in the glee club and walked the halls like a popular kid on campus, greeting other residents and taking questions about Howie.

"He's going into the hospital tomorrow," she told one man. "Hernia operation."

"Howie's young enough to take care of you," he said. "Like I told you, I am not going to go in competition with Howie. He's too nice."

"He's twenty years younger than me," Helen said.

"Well, then he can take care of you."

Howie gave Helen a chance to exercise other muscles. The couple ate all their meals together, sang together in glee club, and watched TV in Helen's room at night. Both remained healthy; Helen, who had always been skinny, put on weight. She wore makeup and jewelry every day and had her hair styled in the facility's salon; she joked about having a crush on one of the visiting doctors. "Things are not so bad for me here," she said. "But there's sadness here. I met some nice people and then they died. I got friendly with them and then they died. I cried a lot. The lady that was next door to me, she was such a nice lady. And what a lovely family she had that used to come see her. When she died I cried so bad. She never bothered anybody. I never bother anybody either."

If John Sorensen battled feelings of uselessness, the challenge for Helen was just the opposite. She felt needed by two people, and, as she was quick to admit, she needed both of them. Howie's and Zoe's needs were complicated and often at war with each other, but both needed her to do the one thing they all knew she couldn't, which was to stay the way she was, without decline. "I don't know what I would do without my mother," Zoe said one day in Helen's room. "That's all I have. She was a tough lady. She's gotten softer." With Helen, "soft" was a relative term.

Helen liked to tell the story of Zoe catching her and Howie in bed together. They were just watching TV, she said, nothing more. "He stays on his side, and I stay here, all the way at the end. 'Get out,' she says to Howie, 'and go to your room.' And he went. I don't care. I'm older than her. I was her age; she was never mine."

Zoe was quick to say that she objected because Helen's twin bed was too narrow for two people, and that she didn't want her mother to fall out and get hurt. But another day, when Helen mentioned sex in conversation, Zoe said, "I don't want to hear about that."

"It's like role reversal," Zoe said. "It's the sandwich generation. I take care of her. She took care of me all these years. I don't do it out of guilt. I do it because she was a great mother. I went with her on a field trip last year and it was the best feeling. I go home and say I'm so happy she's here and she's happy."

She also had other worries, reasonable, I thought, especially once her mother started talking about marrying Howie. If they got married, Howie would be in line to make medical decisions for Helen, and Zoe didn't think he was as capable as she. Also, she said, taking care of Howie slowed her mother down and required a lot of her energy. "She's afraid to say something's bothering her," Zoe said. "But she's never afraid to say, Howie needs his cup of coffee. She's a nurturer, but she doesn't care enough for herself, which was a problem all her life."

"Get her out of here," Helen said.

"I'm just saying, you care more about other people than yourself, and that's part of the problem."

So Helen had two people to manage, both important to her and committed to her, but locked in irreconcilable competition. When Zoe took Helen out for her birthday or holidays, they would leave Howie behind. Since Howie rarely had visitors of his own, it hurt Helen to leave him. "I felt so bad that he didn't come with me," Helen said after a birthday outing. "I didn't feel like going." Zoe said she didn't see the need to include Howie, and didn't know if she could manage both of them. For Helen, Howie's needs were part of the attraction. At her age, it felt good to be essential to someone, providing something he couldn't get from anyone else.

There were parallels. Helen pressed the staff to do more for Howie; Zoe did the same for Helen. Helen disapproved of Zoe's boyfriends when she was young; Zoe now returned the favor. Neither woman backed down readily.

"Be a little nicer to him," Helen said one day. "A little warmer."

Zoe had heard it before. "I'm not here for anybody but my mother," she said. "I'm very happy that you have somebody that shares your life with you, who makes you happy. I'm not going to sit here and say this guy's not for you. He's a very nice man. But I have nothing to do with a nice man. I have everything to do with my mother. It could be any man. I'm here for a short time with her."

Conversations with Helen often returned to themes of loss: her mother, who died nearly a half century ago; residents at the nursing home who showed her kindness when she first moved in; the son from whom she was estranged. "I cried," she said when discussing any of these losses. She worried, as well, about cognitive loss, that she might carry on but not be the person she believed herself to be. Set against these losses, her continuing relationship with Howie was a blow for permanence. Not everything disappears, their relationship seemed to say. Being old didn't have to mean losing what was important to you; sometimes it meant finding it and hanging on to it. Stasis was good;

progress, which dominates our values when we're younger and looking forward to the changes ahead, meant far less to a ninety-year-old for whom the future promised lost friends or faculties. She lived for what she had at the moment.

In July Howie finally had the operation to repair his hernia, which had originally been scheduled for three months earlier. The delay gave Howie more time to worry about it and Helen more time to tell him to buck up, it was just a hernia operation. It also gave Helen more time to let her fears run wild. Any surgery had the potential to upset the status quo. She played it both ways. Once, when she thought Howie was going in for the operation, Helen said she cried all night worrying about him. Here was a reason to be married, she said. If they were married, she could stay in the hospital with Howie, and return to the nursing home with him.

The worrying also affirmed her place as Howie's other half, especially when others asked her about him or how she was feeling. She wasn't just an old woman playing out her last years; she had an essential role in the life of another. Marrying Howie — disrupting the daily routines they'd established over their six years together — was

248

less important than knowing she was in position to marry him. As long as the potential was there, she was getting what she needed and more: not getting married kept the prospect of marriage always in the foreground, never buried beneath the banal domestic details of choosing linens or making guest lists.

The hernia operation went smoothly, and by the time I saw them two weeks later, Helen was again talking about marriage, though more distantly than before. Maybe yes, maybe no, it was a lot to think about. In the meantime, she had a bone to pick with Howie, who hadn't called her after the operation as he had promised.

"Friday morning everyone came to tell me, Howie's home," she said. "So I marched right into his room. I always go into his room when I wake up, before I get my medics. Sometimes I hop in his bed."

"Right," Howie said. "You can include that in the article."

"I said, 'Why didn't you call me? Why didn't you let me know?' I didn't give him a chance to say anything."

Didn't you give him a big kiss? I asked.

"I sure did."

So what was there to learn from Helen? She

249

seemed to make life difficult for herself and the people around her. But as the year went on, I saw that I had this exactly wrong. For the people she cared about most, Zoe and Howie, she made life infinitely richer. If she were simply compliant, as many nursing homes expect of their residents — and many adult children think they want of their elderly parents — she would be far less a factor in their lives. As Howie made Helen feel needed, Helen did the same for Zoe. By not getting married, and not saying she wouldn't, she got what she most wanted from both of them. When I ran this by Helen, late in the year, she said I was reading too much into things. She just knew that she loved Howie and Zoe both, and wished they were nicer to each other.

Yet somehow she had figured it out. Her life had presented her with a choice, and instead of choosing one or the other she chose both. She wasn't playing the two against each other so much as scheduling them in different slots — Zoe in daily phone calls and long weekly visits, and Howie throughout the day. For the years remaining to her she didn't need to resolve the conflict, just to accept it. Her daughter, she acknowledged, was too important to fight with. "She's all I got," Helen said. So at the end of a year of talking about getting married, she and Howie were no closer. It was just an idea — an understanding between them — that brought them closer together. They didn't need to actually do it.

Here was a lesson that had nothing to do with being old. Too often we think that if only we undo the impediments to our happiness, we can be truly happy. But there are always more impediments, more reasons not to be happy now. Helen chose instead to embrace the life she had. She didn't resent her daughter's meddling or feel sorry for herself because she wasn't getting married; she didn't magnify her unmet desires by treating them as a punishment. They were life, her life. Impediments are the circumstances in which we find happiness.

The lesson of Helen was in finding happiness within turmoil, not thinking she could only be happy once it was resolved. She wasn't waiting for external circumstances to bring her contentment. Being satisfied with her life, getting the most of it, meant being satisfied now, not sacrificing the present for a future that might never happen. If her world was small, she was productive and loved within it. Which is where she wanted to be in the last chapter of her life, and a lesson for those of us who are not there yet:

Fulfillment need not be what's just around the corner. In the end, wisdom lies in finding it in the imperfect now.

Eleven:
The Lessons of Ruth
"MAYBE I HAVE DONE SOMETHING RIGHT."

When Judy wants me to hold on to her when we're walking, I kind of pull away, because most of the time I do it by myself, so why should I lean on her now? But sometimes it feels good when she's there for me. Emotionally and physically. It's a good feeling.

— Ruth Willig, ninety-one

The first time Ruth Willig had to uproot her life for her age was in 2009, around the time of her eighty-sixth birthday. She was living alone in a two-story townhouse in Edison, New Jersey, still driving a car, attending events with friends at the nearby Jewish Community Center. She was doing fine, mostly, but a few small things had started to break the wrong way. A smoke detector in her home went off for no apparent reason, and the electrician couldn't fix it, so she disconnected it. Water from the pump in her basement started to seep back indoors. She fell while trying to stand on a stool. "I was being stubborn," she said. "I grabbed something and missed and I went down. But I never broke anything." There were other falls as well, none serious, but she was all alone in the house, climbing stairs whenever she needed to do anything. She'd already had two heart attacks and had bad circulation in one leg. Her four children, middle-aged and still in the area, gathered for a talk about Mom.

"They wanted me to get out of there," she said. "I knew I was getting old. But I was on my own, making my own decisions." She argued against leaving, but her children held firm, and she made the difficult transition to an assisted living facility in Park Slope, Brooklyn, near her oldest daughter, Judy. Five years later, when the facility's owners decided to sell the place for luxury apartments, she had to do it again, this time in concession to the real estate market, not her age. When I met her she was still bitter about the move.

She described these disruptions several times over the year, the last time on a beautiful August day at the New Jersey shore, three months before her ninety-second birthday, as a blistering midday heat softened into a gift of an afternoon. She was staying with her two daughters in the top half of a rented beach house, and the break from their Brooklyn lives — from Ruth's assisted living facility and her daughters' jobs — took the edge off the day. Which is to say, they only snapped at one another a little, and only with obvious affection. Ruth's two sons were actively involved in her life, but as in many families, the bulk of the caregiving fell to her daughters, who never married or had children. The three women were contemplating a walk on the boardwalk, which was down two flights of stairs. Ruth loved getting out in the salt air, but those stairs were a challenge.

"The only problem is, the more I'm out, the more I realize I'm old," she said. "They're talking about [returning] next year. I'm thinking, oh boy." Already she couldn't walk on the sand, and she didn't like the idea of being pushed in a beach wheelchair, which Judy tried to persuade her wasn't really a wheelchair. "It's a chair with wheels," Judy said. At the staircase, when the daughters offered her a hand, Ruth shook them off. "This is an argument we have," she said: "Which is better, for me to go down the stairs first or with you in front helping me."

Judy didn't think this was an argument.

"You say, 'Leave me alone, I'll go down myself,' so that's what we do," she said.

"No you don't," Ruth said.

At the bottom of the stairs, Judy asked her mother if her legs hurt, and Ruth said that they always hurt. Then she said of her daughters, "I'm so fortunate to have them with me. I have wonderful support. And these are not the only two. What could be better? Sometimes I get too much attention. My husband and I did something right."

And so it went, my year with Ruth. She clung to her independence, not giving ground to the assisted living facility or to her children, not wanting to use a walker. She declined her children's offers to manage her finances. At the same time, she was grateful when Judy took her to doctors' appointments or when any of the four visited. "When Judy wants me to hold on to her when we're walking, I kind of pull away," Ruth said, "because most of the time I do it by myself, so why should I lean on her now? But sometimes it feels good when she's there for me. Emotionally and physically. It's a good feeling."

Ruth's conversation over the year tended to fall along two lines. On the one hand, she talked about things *happening to* her, especially as she got older. These stories were almost always of loss. Losing her home was something that happened to her, as were declines in her health and mobility. She'd had to leave her friends from the old building; she couldn't paint like she used to. Several friends died within months of their eviction, and Ruth blamed their deaths on the trauma of having to move. At both facilities she lost her privacy and the ability to set her own schedule. She ate her meals according to the facility's schedule, and chose from the options dictated by the staff. The worst part was that these losses presaged more substantial losses to come, a last chapter characterized by ever-diminishing autonomy and control.

Her other line of conversation focused on things she did for herself. These conversations were always upbeat. She took pride in mastering new skills on the computer, and was always telling me about books she was reading. When she had to leave the Park Slope facility, she joined a protest outside the building with a hand-lettered sign that read OUR PARENTS DESERVE BETTER THAN THIS. She attended a writing class in the new building — a first for her — and discovered some interesting neighbors. Even small things, like ironing her clothes or balancing her checkbook, were victories worth mentioning. If she dwelled on past memories, they were of things she did for herself: raising her four children, attending square dance classes with her husband, caring for her mother or sister. When she remembered setbacks, she also remembered how she overcame them. For Ruth, the sorrows of old age were the things that happened to her, and the joys were the things she did for herself.

Most days, her losses were more on her mind. Psychologists and behavioral economists call this tendency "loss aversion," meaning we place greater value on things we lose than things we gain — even if they're the same things. Ruth loved the old home more when she lost it than when she lived there. If you were to round up a hundred people some morning, give half of them a cookie and the other half a dollar bill, then later in the day offer each a deal — to those who got the cash, a chance to use it to buy a cookie, and to those who got the cookie, a chance to sell it for a dollar — most would reject the deal. Those who got the cookie in the morning would value its loss at more than a dollar, and those who got the dollar would value its loss more highly than the gain of a cookie. This tendency makes young people overrate the losses of old age, and think they can't live without the capabilities they have now. Older people, for whom loss is a part of daily life, don't have this luxury; they either learn to live with decline or they're sunk.

But over the year, Ruth revealed a third line of conversation, involving the support network of her family. With them Ruth was both subject and object, the doer and the done to. "I tell Judy I'm the child she never had," she said one day. "And we have a special relationship, which is wonderful. But sometimes she tends to treat me like — I don't want to put it in a bad way, because she is very caring. They're all very devoted." When her children were younger, the more Ruth did for them, the fuller her life was. Now she was discovering that the complement was also true: as she aged, the more her children did for her, the more satisfaction they got out of it. And she could still do things for them as well.

She took on a family role she never expected to play. She had been the youngest of four siblings, and a rebel in her youth, defying her parents to train for service in Israel after college. Now she was the last survivor from her generation, and the one who kept up with various branches of the family. It gave her a sense of purpose that often eluded her in the assisted living facility, where all she really had to do was show up for meals. Her only regret was that some of her in-laws chose not to stay in contact.

"I'm the matriarch, the last one," Ruth said. "I feel good about it, that they're all responsive to me. I feel proud in a way. I'm in touch with almost all my nieces and nephews, except my husband's family. I feel very happy about that. Maybe I have done something right." The role meant she was still giving something to her family in return for all they gave her. When she had a ninetieth birthday party the year before I met her, relatives flew in from Michigan and California.

It was a system in which everyone both gave and received. If it was demanding, none wanted it not to be; all sides knew that Ruth would rely on her children more and more over time, and that this was not a failure but a success, something to be envied. The relationships had their tensions, but these were nothing new.

"It doesn't change," Judy said one day at the nonprofit organization she runs, Heights and Hills, which provides services to low-income older people, including Fred Jones.

"We yell at each other. But it's sort of a song and dance. You reach a certain point in life when Mom's a finished product, I'm a finished product. Yeah, we occasionally get on each other's nerves, we bicker. But it doesn't mean anything, and we all recognize that. Families do that."

Judy rejected the notion that parents and their children switch roles in old age. "Your parent is your parent and always going to be your parent," she said. "Our roles haven't switched. She's still my mother. And I'm the daughter. She never lets me forget that, and I don't forget it. If *only* she listened to everything I told her to do. Parenting a child and caring for an older person are very different. You're enabling the child to go off and fly. With a parent, it's often the opposite."

For Ruth, though, there were questions: how much to give up before it became too much loss, how much to rely on her children before it ate into the lives she had worked to give them. Part of the dread of living too long was that she might become a "burden" to her children, she said, though she would never have considered her children a burden when they were young and depended on her. As much as she valued self-reliance, with her family this ran up against other virtues, like generosity or reciprocity. Instead of insisting on independence, she was trying to navigate being *inter*dependent, which meant accepting help with gratitude.

Interdependence was a balancing act. The children wanted to do all they could for her without sacrificing their own lives; at the same time, they wanted Ruth to maintain as much control of her life as she could without being unsafe. She wanted to assert her autonomy yet still accept help from her children. She needed to feel she was doing things for herself and others. Yet it pleased her that her children were willing to do so much, even as she told them not to. The lines between too much and enough were subtle and changing. Tomorrow she might not see as well or might make a mistake with her checkbook; the children might have crises of their own to manage. Theirs was a relationship that sociologists call "intimacy at a distance," which required constant vigilance and reassessment. What didn't change was that they needed each other.

Back at the beach house, Ruth moved to sit down, and when Judy held the chair for her, Ruth told her to knock it off. "See, this is what she does," Ruth said, sitting down without help. Neither woman pushed it. This was why they had come to the beach, to be together in all their armor. I envied them.

The Willigs were a stubborn, fractious, and supportive clan, and I was jealous of the crusty warmth with which Ruth's children attended to her. My family had prized independence above all other values. My father, who had almost no contact with his family in Alabama, set the tone. We stood on our own two feet, pulled ourselves up by our bootstraps, the whole nine. We delivered newspapers and raked leaves and bussed tables; we maxed out student loans to contribute to our college ed. But your virtues are also your flaws: we were the family who didn't help each other. We were suspicious of attachment and gave affection warily, if at all. I don't remember ever hearing my father complain — about his health, the TV reception, our finances, my mother's cooking. Complaint was a kind of dependency, because it shifted some of your load to others. My parents had both fled communities where family ties were strong and long, for New York City, where individuals were autonomous and self-invented. We performed the rituals of family the way some people attend church, because it's the right thing to do, rather than because they feel the spirit. It worked fine until it didn't. Then my mother was on her own, with three sons who thought being on your own was the goal of human existence. We weren't opposed to family warmth; we just didn't speak the language, and didn't know where to learn it.

Put a gun to my head and it would never occur to me to invite my mother for a week at the beach.

If you were to construct an endgame for a satisfying old age, you might begin with family support. But how to get there? Helen's daughter, Zoe, provided one model; John's niece Anne another. They were take-charge personalities who took charge, each willing to make any sacrifice to keep Helen or John going. The Willigs posed a different model of support. They formed a network in which Ruth was a contributing partici-pant, giving as she received. They weren't all lovey all the time, but they didn't have to be. There were unstated rules: Ruth couldn't scold her children too hard for offering to help her, and the children couldn't take of-fense if she did. The arrangement allowed Ruth to demand independence when it was possible, a shoulder to lean on when it wasn't.

At her work, Judy gives her staff a passage

from Wendy Lustbader, the mental health counselor and writer, to help them understand the pitfalls of caregiving relationships. Lustbader writes:

> Receiving is much harder than giving, but this fact is seldom recognized in mainstream American society. Dependent people are often deprived of chances to give, finding that they must endure a state of almost constant relinquishment and passivity. Consequently, the person receiving help accumulates a debt to the other and must bear the weight of feeling beholden day in and day out. There are few means through which the person can pay back a caregiver for rides to the doctor, help with medical bill paperwork, handling loads of laundry, and check-up telephone calls — the list of favors owed can be immense. The dependent person may yearn for something useful to do, only to be admonished, "Don't worry, we'll take care of everything."

For family caregivers, Lustbader notes the hidden resentments that arise from the relationship's asymmetry. Caring is mutual; caregiving can be all one way, a drain on both parties. But acknowledging the underlying dynamic can take away its sting. "The reward for recognizing resentment," Lustbader writes, "is enjoying the ill person's company again."

At first I thought there were lessons for my mother in Ruth's experience: that if she wanted satisfaction in her old age, she could generate it by doing more for herself or others. It didn't have to be a major project: volunteer to read to the blind; cook a simple meal or make coffee for a neighbor or two. Think of your life as what you do, not what happens to you. But as I observed Ruth and her family, I realized that the deeper lessons were for me. I needed to rethink my relationship with my mother — and, by extension, with my own eventual old age. I was too quick to think of her as simply dependent, and dependence as simply a problem — small now, but sure to grow. Ruth's family, by contrast, did more for her by making room for her to do things for them. It wasn't always smooth, but it beat the guilt and resentment that made my relationship with my mother so draining. If all I was doing was giving, and begrudgingly, then I was just digging a deeper hole.

A lesson of Ruth was that there was a different way. Of the six elders, she was the most assertively independent, but also the one who got the most emotional support from her family. She relied on this. Some of my impatience with my mother, I realized, was really directed at her comfort with being dependent. Ruth showed that there was life beyond independence. For all her will to be self-sufficient, the best parts of her life were those in which she relied on others and gave thanks for it.

Over the year, I began to see my mother less as a project — one at which I would ultimately fail — and more as a pleasant dinner companion, someone who had seen the world and had thoughts about it. This she could still give. She was funny; she knew things I didn't, including things about the world I came from, and the one that awaited me down the line. Not that we became all lovey, or even as lovey as the Willigs. But spending time together didn't have to be all for her benefit, a sacrifice I made in the midst of my busy life. It could just be time together. It wasn't my job to fix Mom or make her appreciate her life. That was a choice she could make or not make. As I started to dial back my sense of fulfilling an obligation, I enjoyed my visits with her more. My mother has a great, dry sense of humor. I left visits to her apartment feeling upbeat rather than worn down.

Sometimes, waiting on the elevated subway platform near Ruth's home, I wondered whether anyone would support me like Ruth's family when I got older. But as the year went along, I started to think more about how much support I was already getting, how little responsibility I bore for most of the good in my life. I was in better health than Ruth, but we all have limitations at any age, and our lives everywhere are built on the help of others: the people who built roads or invented alphabets, the colleagues who fix the photocopier or their ancestors who discovered pi. Help is everywhere — it is vanity to think we're compromised by it. As Barack Obama said on the campaign trail, "If you've got a business — you didn't build that. Somebody else made that happen." Vast forces in the universe had conspired to enable me to awaken in my bed rather than as a widow with five children in Aleppo. Why not embrace this mutual dependency and aid?

If this was thinking like an old person, I gradually started to open to it. Instead of fighting for my way at work, I thanked my editors for making my writing better; I asked advice instead of feeling I should know all the answers. I called my mother more often, also my son, with questions rather than answers. What did they need from me? Anything I did for them would benefit me at least as much as them, because interdependency benefits all parties. Ruth had learned to accept help, and her life was better for it. So could mine be. Of course I have bad days, and more serious ones await, but a lesson of Ruth was that I won't face them alone, that there are forces lined up with me. It didn't mean the hardships won't be real; it meant that I have resources to survive them, and that these resources, more than any hardships, define my life.

One day in Ruth's apartment, she described a recent incident that struck her as a fine act of self-assertion. By then I had published a couple of articles about the elders, and the management of Ruth's building was pressing her to alert them in advance of my visits, which she resented. "What are they worried about?" she said. These were the battles she found herself fighting. "Yesterday someone knocked on the door in the middle of the afternoon," she said. "And I said, nobody's supposed to do that. I'm very strong on keeping my privacy as much as I can, but it's hard in a place like this."

The incident she described started at lunch the day before, when a woman at a nearby table, a few years older than she, dropped her head and blacked out where she sat. The woman was just out, Ruth said. The staff took her out of the dining room, apparently unconscious. Ruth assumed she had gone to the hospital, which was always a cause for worry. But when Ruth returned for dinner a few hours later, she was surprised to see the woman at her usual table. "She said, 'I decided it wasn't time to go. I refused to go to the hospital. I got a couple years yet.' " Ruth paused to let that sink in, a ninetysomething woman taking control of her life like that. "Isn't that something?"

With her children, it was harder to know how far to assert herself. She had always been the one helping them over hurdles, keeping them safe from tigers. Now she knew she would depend on them more and more; it was just a matter of time. "I'm known when I get out of the car to push them away," she said. "I did. Now I'm not as self-sufficient as I was. I see changes, which is upsetting. My physical dependence — I haven't been out for days except for appointments, and that bothers me, because I would love to go out. Part of it is, walking with the walker puts me in a class that I don't want to be in. Hard to explain. Sometimes we all parade with the walkers and I say, 'Oh my God, what's happening?' It's like *The Producers,* the show, when he's trying to get the older women to contribute, and there's the parade of walkers. I see myself in that way. I don't like that portrayal. But that's me. Judy keeps telling me I have a very good memory, which I do. I'm glad of that. So that hasn't changed too much. But this hand shakes a lot, I have trouble writing. Eating soup. I pick up the cup and drink it. And I'm slow. Like yesterday I finally took care of some paperwork. Takes me a long time."

My year with Ruth, then, was one of watching her adjust. The process was different than it might have been with a younger person in a new setting. She never released her anger at having to leave the old building, or at the invasions to her privacy in the new one. She didn't make close new friends, as she had in the old building, and didn't discover charms in the new neighborhood. In the limited time left to her, she didn't feel she had to bend herself to things she didn't like. When the news filled with stories about Caitlyn Jenner and transgender identity, Ruth didn't object — she just didn't relate, and didn't feel obligated to. "Transgender, what will they think of next?" she said. "Sometimes I'm glad I'm ninety-one.

I'm finished. That way I'm glad I'm ninety-one, because maybe I won't have to deal with that."

The things that irritated her at the start of the year — things that happened to her — still irritated her at the end. But she gradually started to feel at home in the new facility. "I'm trying harder," she said one day toward the end of the summer. The sun poured into her living room, which looked out onto the salt water of Sheepshead Bay. A pink geranium she'd brought from her old building bloomed ostentatiously in the window. "I'm not giving up," she said. "Not yet. When I was complaining a lot about this place — which I was, because the change was so hard — my son Bruce would come here and say 'Mom, you look out and you can see the water.' And I do look out at the water when I wake up. It's pretty. So I can almost call it home." When she thought about what could improve her life now, she said, "I don't know what anyone can do for me anymore. I think it's up to me at this point. The activities here, most of them do not interest me. So I make my own entertainment. Which is fine. I'm really not complaining about that. I don't need a lot of people."

Days brought small victories: learning to

program a DVR; ironing a shirt when it would have been easier to let it stay wrinkled; keeping her apartment clean without unwanted help from the building staff; getting around without the walker on short trips. She took up shopping from catalogs and online rather than let her children shop for her.

And weekends brought contact with her family, especially her daughters. With her children, she could see herself as she was in many stages of her life, not just as a nonagenarian who had trouble walking. She was the mother she had always been and the daughter Judy never had. One day, when she questioned the point of living so long, she remembered that her grandson was participating in a mock congress at his high school, and that she was alive to share his excitement. "When I think that, I think, Look at my grandson, look what he's doing. So I'm excited about that." This was enough to keep her going. She lived for what she had and loved, not for what she lost.

Even as her social network tightened, she never said she was lonely. The relationships she held on to were meaningful and productive, and she had managed to filter out a lot of the relationships that vex people at any age. Life was short; find the people who really matter, and the relationships that allow you to thrive. With her children and extended family, she had gifts to offer that no one else could. She was useful to them, and they appreciated her. If she couldn't walk much, that wasn't what they needed from her.

"So what do I actually do for her?" Judy said one day. "Not a whole lot. Provide her with emotional support. I love my mother. We all do. Help her with the computer sometimes. She's fiercely independent. That's really important to her, and we all honor that. So I haven't taken away anything from her, except driving, and she gave that up. She said she didn't know what she could give anymore. She gives what she always gave, she gives us love. She's the backbone of our family. So she doesn't cook for us anymore."

Over the course of the year, Ruth stayed mostly healthy, but her energy level dropped, and when winter returned, with the short days, she stopped going outside and spent more time alone in her apartment, reading or playing FreeCell on her computer. She noticed that her winning percentage was going down. The year was hard on her, and the next would be harder.

But the rewards she enjoyed were those of

her choosing. As the year came to a close, this was true of all the elders. They had little say in the hardships that came their way — the new aches or health problems, the days on end when no one called or visited — but the satisfactions were of their own making. It took some effort. Yet each found a way to it.

Some days the effort was too much, or the pain, or the loss, and those were bad days or weeks. Those were the old age we've grown to dread, the one that happens to people. A lesson from my year among the oldest old is that this old age is not inevitable or immutable. We each will have some say in the matter, at least until we don't. Ruth, when she turned ninety, got excited because she felt she had put in a good life, and now she could make her exit. She wasn't interested in reaching one hundred, like other people she knew. "I felt that I had achieved a certain landmark," she said. "The family came, we had a party. The rest is a bonus."

This is a good summation for the arc of life at any age. You never know when the bonus round is going to kick in, but you can prepare for it. In the meantime, whether we're twenty-five or eighty-five, we can choose to live in the things that warm us —

in love, humor, compassion, empathy, a supportive arm — not because they make life easy, but because they do the most for us when life is hard. As Ruth said, after another tough year, "I wouldn't have felt bad if I had to go. But I guess I'm glad I didn't."

TWELVE:
THE LESSONS OF JONAS
"YOU HAVE TO TRUST YOUR ANGELS."

> My ideal, how I would like to be when I'm
> one hundred, is this old guy who used to
> come visit my father. He used to climb on
> the roof of our house and stand on his
> head on the chimney. When I asked my
> father how old he was, he said he was one
> hundred. So that's my ideal.
> — Jonas Mekas, ninety-two

Early in my year with the elders, Jonas
invited me to a one-woman show at a tiny
second-floor theater in the East Village.
Jonas, who at ninety-two was the oldest of
the bunch, periodically sent me e-mails like
this, last-minute notices that he was going
to read at a poetry club or front a bassist
and drummer at a bar on Avenue A or speak
at a conference in Berlin. His regular dive
bar had recently been eaten by New York's
real estate boom, and the Brooklyn music
space where he liked to sing and blow an
untutored horn had succumbed to the

march of "squares" into Williamsburg, so Jonas's nightlife had taken on a one-off character, without fixed ports of call. The hurly-burly suited him, but he missed the places where he could just show up and know he'd find company.

The show in the East Village turned out to be a one-act monologue called "That's How Angels Arranged," part of a series drawn verbatim from interviews with people who'd made a mark on the neighborhood. The woman playing Jonas was a twenty-something named Lillian Rodriguez, wearing a beret and zipper jacket in place of the blue French workman's jacket Jonas had on whenever I saw him. She replicated his Lithuanian accent pretty well, I thought, though Jonas and his son, Sebastian, who was thirty-three, thought otherwise.

"I landed in New York like an empty sponge," she said. "And I was twenty-seven, so that was crucial, really." And she was off, in a digressive monologue that moved from Lithuania to Nazi Germany to Brooklyn to the Lower East Side to life as an elder in New York's underground art world. Jonas had said many of the things from the monologue in our conversations, but it was a revelation to hear them coming from the mouth and body of a woman nearly seventy

278

years his junior. Her body language was that of a young woman, quite different from Jonas's, but it suited the words and ideas uncannily. She played the old man as a young spirit, which is how anyone who knew Jonas saw him.

Toward the end of the monologue, Rodriguez-as-Jonas compared her life to a savory stew. Individual moments of that life, like ingredients in the stew, might taste terrible or be too hot to eat on their own — "you can't take them," she said — but once they were all mixed together, you wouldn't want to be without any of them. "So," she said, "I wouldn't change anything."

Watching the performance put Jonas in a reflective mood, because here was someone with vastly different experiences narrating his life, a role he usually assumed. Like her, Jonas often seemed to be performing a part he had written for himself, becoming his persona by saying the words. Afterward, we walked quietly in search of a drink and a place to talk, passing a bar where Jonas, living in absolute penury at the time, had started screening other people's movies in the early 1950s. There was a light drizzle in the air, and the glow from the streetlights danced on the wet pavement.

"People say 'Oh, it's so sad through what

you had to go,' " Jonas said, going back to the story from the show. "No, I'm happy that I was uprooted, because I was dropped in New York in the most exciting period, when all the classical arts had reached culmination, like Balanchine and Martha Graham, and something else was coming in. I caught Marlon Brando and Tennessee Williams and Miller; I saw the end of the old when I came in forty-nine, and I saw the beginning of the new, John Cage and Buckminster Fuller and the Living Theater and the Beat Generation. And I was a sponge for all of it."

We ducked into his favorite French bistro, where there were photographs of him on the walls.

Jonas Mekas was born on Christmas Eve of 1922, and grew up with four brothers and a sister in the small farm village of Semeniskiai, in northeastern Lithuania. He once counted the village population at twenty-two families and ninety-eight heads. He was sickly as a child, and the family farm's needs caused him to fall behind in school, but in his teens he made up five years in one semester. In a family of poets, Jonas developed a poetic voice deeply rooted in the Lithuanian language and countryside, mak-

280

ing up words to capture moods and scenes. On the farm he ran distances with his younger brother Adolfas and developed a knack for standing on his head while riding horseback, and marveled at a hardy visitor who used to climb on the Mekas family roof and do headstands on the chimney. "He was my ideal," Jonas said. "When I asked my father how old he was, he said he was one hundred. So that's my ideal. And actually it's after that that I picked up standing on my head."

If you could bottle the life force that is Jonas, you could spare the world a whole lot of misery. He doesn't defy aging so much as fulfill its potential, marshaling all his past into a present only available to someone who has lived a long life. He took his first photograph at age fifteen — Soviet soldiers and tanks rolling into his village — started an anti-Nazi underground newspaper when he was twenty, immigrated to New York when he was almost twenty-seven, made his first autobiographical film at forty-six, launched his website at eighty-three, and at ninety-two presided over a massive installation of his work at a Burger King in Venice, Italy, during the 2015 Biennale. At ninety-three, his biggest complaint was a corn in his right foot.

A hazard of living so long, he said, was that each year there were fewer people who could remember the eras that he lived through, so he was always being called upon to tell the old stories. "They ask me, how come you still remember it all?" he wrote to me in an e-mail. "Why not, I say, it was my life, it's normal to remember it all unless one messes up one's life, one's body when one is young. What keeps you young? they ask me. And I say, it's Wine, Women and Song. But at the same time I am a monk, I live like a monk. . . . But that is very normal! It's not normal not to sing, not to dance, not to like poetry, not to be interested in matters of spirit! I am a very very normal case. And I am happy. Happiness is a normal state."

Jonas often said he wasn't a thinking person, and that ideas were the worst things in the world, because people who had ideas acted on them — as he had witnessed in Soviet-occupied Lithuania and in Nazi Germany. So he tried to move wholly on instinct, waking up with no plans for the day, pointing his camera as he would direct his eyes, letting the scene come to him. "I'm not a very introspective person," he said. "When you come from a farmer's background — village life — people live, they don't analyze themselves. It's more communal, more like being, living, communicating with friends, neighbors. Of course self-analysis and introspection came in later as I progressed and left the village. But still, by nature I'm not analyzing myself, even if I'm being diaristic in video and writing. It's self-centered but if you read [the diaries of] Anaïs Nin and Henry Miller, it's very introspective and convoluted, but I'm not that type of person, so my diaries are not that personal."

A paradox of this way of living is that it requires an exceptionally solid sense of purpose and direction. Otherwise your actions become random noise. Jonas's values were straightforward and unchanging: he liked music and nature and celebrating with friends, and he preferred art and beauty to ugliness and existential despair. His best-known poems, *Idylls of Semeniskiai,* written in a displaced persons camp in Germany, are reveries for rustic life in Lithuania, where "old is this rushing of rain down the bush branches, / the droning of grouse in the red dawn of summer — / old is this our talking." Having this compass meant he never stopped working but also never started. "I'm just doing," he said often. Not thinking or filming or writing — just living.

"When I grew up on a farm we did not consider that we were working," he said one day, when I arrived at his loft to find him sorting through loose frames from his films for an exhibition in Paris. "We were just doing what had to be done that day. We had to plant certain things, to milk certain cows. The concept of workers came when the Soviets came in and organized the workers. Suddenly everybody was a worker. But we were not workers until then. So I'm continuing what I was doing when I was growing up: I'm just doing what has to be done."

Another day, he said, "Farmers cultivate different things. I cultivate poetry and the saints, history, beauty, art. That's what I chose."

One of the great mysteries of old age is why some people, like Jonas, continue to grow and thrive long after their peers wind down. If it were easy we'd all do it. Heredity might seem an obvious answer, but it turns out to have less effect than we might think. Studies with Danish twins, among others, have found that genes account for only about one-quarter of our differences in longevity. A history of smoking, trauma, stress, and other factors similarly plays a role, but plenty of stressed-out smokers go on to enjoy fully satisfying third acts, while their yoga-observant peers hit the skids.

"This is the most extraordinary question," said Karl Pillemer of Cornell. "Why do people turn out this way? I don't think we have an answer. Of what we do know, some is exactly what you'd think, and some is surprising."

Drug companies, cosmetics manufacturers, and lifestyle marketers are happy to sell you "anti-aging" or "age-resistant" products to help you "turn back time" or "feel like a kid again," all for the low, low price of as much money as you can afford. But no amount of miracle wrinkle remover will make you Jonas Mekas. The good news is that more useful fixes are closer to hand, and cheaper.

Becca R. Levy, a psychiatrist at Yale, has found striking correlations between people's attitudes toward old age and how they fare in their later years, with effects starting as early as middle age. In one study, those who had more positive views of old age, measured by how they answered the question, "When you think of old persons, what are the first five words or phrases that come to mind?" were 44 percent more likely to recover from a disability than those with negative age stereotypes. In other studies,

Levy and her colleagues found that people with positive views of old age had lower blood pressure, less stress, better physical balance, and were more likely to develop healthy habits and get regular medical care. They also lived an average of seven and a half years longer — a genuine fountain of youth, available without a prescription.

Jonas wasn't immune to negative stereotypes, but he offset these with more positive associations, like the hundred-year-old man who did headstands on the family chimney or the saints who became more venerable with age. To the extent that he avoided the company of boring old farts, it was more because they were boring than because they were old.

"What keeps him alive is that he is an enthusiast," said Johan Kugelberg, fifty, a curator and archivist who in 2017 published a collection of Jonas's writings and photographs called *A Dance with Fred Astaire*. He described Jonas as "the anti-Warhol, Obi-Wan Kenobi to Warhol's Darth Vader. He is my hero because he never succumbs to the dark side. And neither will I, because of Jonas."

Patricia Boyle, a neuropsychologist and researcher at the Rush Alzheimer's Disease Center, a part of Rush University Medical

Center in Chicago, has a name for the life force that keeps people like Jonas going: purpose. Researchers have long observed that older people who feel a sense of purpose in their lives tend to live longer, fuller, and healthier lives than people who don't. The finding is not surprising: people in bad health or with dementia are less likely to feel that what they do makes a difference. So purpose might be an effect of good health rather than the cause.

Boyle and her researchers set out to explore the relationship between purpose and Alzheimer's disease, which is believed to affect one in nine Americans over age sixty-five, and has no effective medical treatment. First, the researchers tested the memories of 1,400 older people over a period of eight years, while also measuring how strongly they felt a purpose in life. To test the latter, the researchers asked participants whether they agreed or disagreed with statements like "Some people wander aimlessly through life, but I am not one of them."

As in previous studies, people who had a purpose in life suffered less memory loss over the eight years of the study than those who didn't. But it was after some had died, and Boyle examined their brains, that the nature of this relationship jumped out at her. Alzheimer's causes cell death and tissue loss in the brain, most likely from the buildup of what are called plaques and tangles. Plaques are clusters of beta-amyloid proteins that form between nerve cells and seem to prevent them from passing signals between synapses. Tangles are twisted protein strands that form within nerve cells and prevent nutrients from reaching the cells, causing the cells to die off.

As participants in the study died, Boyle's team performed autopsies on 246 brains. They found that having a purpose in life seemed to have no effect on whether the brains formed plaques and tangles — a purposeful brain deteriorated at the same rate as one that perceived no meaning in the universe. But when the researchers went back and looked at the memory scores of those identical brains, they found wide differences in performance. Those with a sense of purpose had deteriorated little in their memory scores — even when the cellular damage in the brain was identical to those with dementia. This suggests that having a purpose doesn't protect you from forming the plaques and tangles that define Alzheimer's, but it seems to prevent or delay the effects. Boyle's explanation is that having a purpose creates a "reserve" that enables some brains to form other pathways to transmit signals and nutrients and remain functional. The stronger the purpose, the more protective it is.

"It has a lifelong benefit, but something unique happens in old age, where being goal-directed helps you stave off bad health outcomes," she said. The good news, she said, is that people at any age can learn to form a purpose in life, either on their own or through simple interventions. Yours might be weak or strong, but you will benefit either way. "Part of it is getting people to sit down and say 'What do I want my life to look like at the end of the day?' " she said. " 'What do I want my mark to be?' If we can move that needle, we believe that can have major public health benefits." Even in people with severe health problems or disabilities, she added, "having a purpose in life lets us look inward to say, How am I going to live my life, what do I want to accomplish?"

The challenge, then, is to find a purpose in life that will sustain you through the latter years. Kickboxing might not be a great choice, but painting, political activity, time with family, or passing along your skills to the next generation can be a reason for living at any age. Practice law, feed the hungry, teach piano, harass your congressman, tell your story. It's your purpose in life: make it a passion, not a hobby.

For Jonas, having a purpose was never an issue. He had a purpose when he twice escaped Nazi work camps, when he fell in love with cinema in a displaced persons camp, and when he applied to resettle in Israel to help build the new state (he was turned down because there was no quota for Lithuanian gentiles). When he got to New York, he threw himself into supporting other filmmakers' work even before he became known for his own. Half a century later the same purpose still drives him, with even more urgency because time is short. But trying to explain where he got it was like explaining why he breathed; he just did.

"Something is in you that propels you," he said one day in his apartment, still basking in a night of watching the U.S. women's soccer team win the World Cup. He was sitting at a table with a stack of old books and a bottle of San Pellegrino water, as Lillian Rodriguez had been for her performance. "It's part of your very essence, what you are," he said. "There is a need. Like, go back to Greeks and muses. How they explained that, the muse enters you at birth or later, music or whatever art, and you have no choice. It becomes part of you. You just have to do it."

During the year I spent with Jonas, he had a clear goal, to raise money to build a library and café at Anthology Film Archives, the theater and archive he started with friends in 1970, which remains the premier spot to see avant-garde films in New York. The café, he believes, is necessary to keep the institution going. Jonas has often given his own money to institutions or other filmmakers over the years, even when he was broke himself. As the filmmaker Stan Brakhage, to whom Jonas gave both financial and moral support, once said about him, "Jonas has many pockets, and all of them are open."

Now he was calling in favors from friends. From Paris he got John Cale to promise a new composition for an Anthology auction; from New York he got Matthew Barney to donate sketches of Jonas. Every few months came an excited e-mail about an artist who was contributing work.

He often spoke about having angels to protect him, even claiming he had photographic proof of their existence. Angels, he said, had enabled him to survive his uprooted years, and to pay the rent in New

York when there was no money coming in. They were the flip side of his purpose in life — a reason not to push too hard or worry about whether he was making headway. He could risk failing or starving because angels would look after him, as they had in truly hard times. "Angels protected us because there was something we still had to do," he said. "Since I don't know why angels saved us, to do what, I don't think about what I have to do, I just do it, hoping that that's what my fate is. If I have any problems that emerge, I say, okay, I will leave it alone for now, let time work on it. I don't dwell on anything that is problematic. I leave it alone and as time goes, very often it straightens out by itself. I say, okay, I cannot deal with it, so you, angels, now it's your job. You work on it and I will do something else. And usually they do it. Trust — that's what I advise if anyone asks. You have to trust your angels."

He added, "I will start to worry when something happens. Why worry when it's not happening? Then why worry when it happens? You deal with it. You waste time worrying and that may never happen what you think. I will deal when it happens, but you don't waste time. Nothing is hopeless. I

don't even know what it means — hopeless."

Instead, he pointed to a motto for living
that he wrote for the designer Agnès B:
"Keep dancing. Keep singing. Have a good
drink and do not get too serious."

Don't worry. Keep singing and dancing.
These are the secondary lessons of Jonas,
which would be enough from most people.
His primary lesson is to maintain a purpose
in life. The unspoken corollary, of course, is
to find a purpose in the first place — starting now.

On a Saturday afternoon in early spring, I
found Jonas in a Greenwich Village jazz
club, the Zinc Bar, seated among a group of
student opera singers from Lithuania. He
was there to read from his unpublished
novella called *Requiem for a Manual Typewriter,* about the bewildering prospect of
trying to decide what to write about. The
students, who were seventeen and eighteen,
were chaperoned by a sixty-five-year-old
émigré named Raminta Lampsatis, who had
lived in exile in Chicago until the fall of the
Soviet Union and now taught in Germany.
For her generation of expatriates, Jonas's
poems about Lithuania were the stuff of
campfire gatherings, where young refugees

felt the pang of their exile and the comfort food of their home language. But for her students, she said, Jonas was something entirely new. "He's their culture," she said. "He's a person for three or four generations."

The group was joined at the table by two New York writers in their seventies, Lynne Tillman and Amy Taubin, whose careers Jonas had helped get started — a typical scattering of ages and backgrounds, with Jonas at the center, a generation older than the next in line. He was drinking a beer and clearly enjoying the company. The students seemed thrilled to sit with a national legend. Bernardas Garbačiauskas, seventeen, a baritone, said that his friends had all asked him whether he planned to see Jonas in New York. For their generation, he said, Jonas's film diaries were a precursor to Instagram or Facebook, invented nearly a half century ago. Far from sitting with an old man, he said, "Jonas Mekas is the future."

As Jonas took the stage, his hand shook, but he read in a wry, confident voice that silenced the room. "I have decided to write a novel that is absolutely about nothing," he read, beginning a tale about finding a roll of computer paper and deciding he needed to write something on it. Like most of his work, the novella took the shape of a diary and spoke in a voice of wonder. "Have you ever thought about how amazing, really amazing, life is?" he read, to laughter from a full house.

This may be the one-sentence essence of what I learned in my year among the oldest old: to shut down the noise and fears and desires that buffet our days and think about how amazing, really amazing, life is. Could I do this? Before the year began, my answer would have been no, that the noise and fears and desires were life itself. But as the year went along I found myself shifting my focus to the quiet beneath the noise — how unlikely the moment was, how each sliver contained a gift that might never return. Maybe this was what it meant to think like an old person. I couldn't live wholly in the moment, because I had a future to think about, but if I had learned anything, it was to live as if this future were finite, and the present all the more wondrous as a result.

Each of the elders arrived at some version of this accommodation, because they couldn't help it: life's changes kept coming at them, whether they wanted them or not. Did they ever think about how amazing, really amazing, life is? Each, I think, was on his or her way. Even as their worlds got smaller, their capacity for amazement did not desert them; little delights were no longer so little. Wonder, too, is a choice you make. Ping found it in the companionship of mah-jongg; Fred found gratitude in waking up each day; Helen found ways to be needed and to need; John found luminous music in the face of death; and Ruth learned to trust her angels, which in her case meant her children.

During the year, I asked each of them whether they thought about death, and whether the thought scared them, and all but Fred Jones said no to the latter. Living too long scared them; dying was the antidote to living too long. A part of the wisdom of their late years was accepting death and aging as part of life. Only the young think they aren't dying, or that aging is something that affects other people.

At the Zinc Bar, Jonas's *Requiem for a Manual Typewriter* ended with his character learning that William Burroughs had died. "So he's gone, too," Jonas read. When I asked later whether he thought about his own death, he said that death was the wrong question. The question was life. "My own end will come when it's ready to come, but I never think about that," he said. "You cannot protect yourself from death." All around him he saw people disengaged from the life they were given. "I grew up with no radio, no electricity, no television, no music, no phonographs. I saw my first movie when I was fourteen. One could live to two hundred. But yet I see some young people, twenty years old, and they seem to be bored already with life, and some of them cannot stand it. That's something else."

The neurologist Oliver Sacks, on learning that he had terminal cancer of the liver, wrote that the nearness of death gave him a sudden clear focus, and no patience for anything inessential. "I cannot pretend I am without fear," he wrote. "But my predominant feeling is one of gratitude. I have loved and been loved; I have been given much and I have given something in return; I have read and traveled and thought and written. I have had an intercourse with the world, the special intercourse of writers and readers. Above all, I have been a sentient being, a thinking animal, on this beautiful planet, and that in itself has been an enormous privilege and adventure." In seven months he was dead.

How can we live in this heightened state all our lives, without the blessing of terminal cancer to remind us that life is a great unearned gift? How can we train our minds to revel in its privilege and adventure? This is the question I kept returning to throughout my year with the elders. Did we really have to wait for word from our oncologist to live as fully as we were capable? It didn't seem so complicated. Yet the thing that should come most easily — to live as if we're going to die — is often the one we most strenuously avoid.

At year's end I asked Jonas whether, having experienced the Soviet occupation of Lithuania and imprisonment by the Nazis, he was an optimist. He took a few stabs at an answer before giving up, then sent an e-mail message the next day. "I would say, that I am applying the 'butterfly wing' theory to my everyday life," he wrote. "It's a kind of moral dictum, moral responsibility to keep in mind that whatever I do this second affects what the next second will be. So I try not to do anything negative, which is my best insurance that the world will be better next second, or at least not worse. But of course, my positive action may be undermined by 100 negative actions of others and so it may mean nothing. But I still have to follow that dictum. You can call it optimism."

We talked again about happiness and what it meant to him. Were older people happier?

Parts of his past were bitter and depressing when he was living them; the sunny reminiscences of his nineties would have seemed insane in his twenties or thirties. After a year together, I understood better that his happiness came not despite his advanced age but through it, because now he could look at his life in its nearly complete state, and savor it for what it gave him, not what he might get in the future. More years, for Jonas, meant more things that he had done right. More movies seen, more books read, more friendships toasted, more thoughts thought, more context he could apply to whatever new he encountered today. Of course older people were happier, he said. "Happiness is to see that all that what you did is working, doing good work, my children are growing up and having their lives beautifully. I see that whatever I did and whatever I'm doing, it's nothing I should feel unhappy about. I feel that whatever I'm doing or did is right, and I feel very good about it. I'm not pushing, I'm listening with an ear always to the angels, and I'm happy."

I remembered an afternoon together earlier in the year, eating herring and boiled potatoes at a Russian café near Anthology. The place was called the Anyway Café, and Jonas joked that he was well in any way.

"My doctor told me yesterday at my yearly checkup that I would be one of those who lived to be one hundred and twenty," he said. "I said, really? He said, the way technology is now, and all the things being invented, I will be among those, and there will be some others. I said thank you. So I said, but that's normal. When people ask me, what's your secret, it's no secret. Only because others, those who are not in my shape at my age, they lead abnormal lives. They eat too much, they drink too much, they do everything too much. Whatever I do is just what's needed, normal. I'm a normal case. All the other people that I meet are not normal."

A square of afternoon sunlight streamed into the cave-like restaurant, burnishing Jonas like a Dutch oil painting, making 120 seem no more outrageous than any of the other normalcies from Jonas's life. Why not? He finished the year largely as he started it, with several book manuscripts calling for his attention and boxes of old film footage that he had abandoned as bad decades ago, now maybe ready to be edited into a film or two. Age had a way of turning disappointment into new discovery. "As time goes," he said, "some of it becomes very rare, like any old photograph that you discover from the nineteenth century — it does not matter if it's art or no art. It's like the art that we have in museums from the second century or fourth century: because it survived we put it in there."

All six elders, I'm happy to say, survived the year, as did my mother, despite her minor heart attack toward the end. As January approached I began to feel separation anxiety because our year was coming to an end. They had carried me through a difficult time and were guiding me through the sweeter one that followed. The year put its marks on them: John was heart-wrenchingly frail, Ping had more frequent lapses in memory, and Fred seemed unlikely to get many chances to wear the purple suit; he still hadn't been to church. But he loved envisioning himself in its purple majesty, and he loved even more that a near stranger had been kind enough to make it a reality — two more reasons to be grateful in a life for which not everyone would give thanks. He still wanted to make it to 110.

So it was with each of them: their joys and pains were the same at the end of the year as they were in the beginning, just further along in their narratives. Now that the year was ending, each considered it to have been worth living, no less so because they hadn't run a marathon or jumped out of an airplane. Ruth saw her grandchildren move another year toward adulthood; Helen had another year with Howie; John enjoyed another Thanksgiving with his friends from Fire Island. Fred made new friends and saw himself looking sharp; Ping congratulated herself on her resourcefulness and luck, living a rich life with almost no money. Jonas did it all. Each relished time with relatives; all complained about the food — a New York prerogative if ever there was one.

These may seem paltry compensations for all the blows the elders took over the year, a bad deal dressed up in wishful sentiment. Ezekiel Emanuel, in his essay about choosing not to prolong his life after seventy-five, dreaded particularly "the constricting of our ambitions and expectations," until a once-full "life comes to center around sitting in the den reading or listening to books on tape and doing crossword puzzles." Small pleasures, whatever their virtues, may not be worth sticking around for, especially when it hurts just to get out of bed in the morning.

But another way to look at them, invoking Lars Tornstam's concept of gerotranscendence, is as products of highly mature thought. It takes seventy or eighty or ninety years to learn the value of another sunrise or a visit from a surly grandchild — to appreciate how amazing, really amazing, life is. They only seem paltry because we haven't lived long enough to see their value, or survived enough losses to know how surmountable most losses are. Simple gifts can be as rewarding as more elaborate ones, and there's no rule that a life of daily mah-jongg in a fluorescent-lit community room is less fulfilling than one of high-stakes baccarat in Monte Carlo. James Joyce's *Ulysses* concerns a single day in a humdrum town; *War and Peace* spans an epoch and revels in great passions and pageantry. But no one would say that one realm is richer than the other; they just tap different ways of looking at the world. Whether the lens is a telescope or a microscope, the wonder lies always in the eye of the beholder.

Was Fred Jones right to give thanks for another day, or was he a deluded old man too compromised to know better? Were my mother and John Sorensen right to want release from their lives, or just too rigid to appreciate the advantages they enjoyed? When I visited John I usually reminded him that his aide, Scott, was coming the next day, or Markus or Alex, or his niece, Anne,

303

and didn't he want to stay around for that? He did, of course — he just didn't want to have years and years to get through afterward. His answer remained the same even later, when he got very sick. A Joycean day was a knowable quantity and a gift; a Tolstoyan era was a great dark unknown. As long as time was finite, John could delight in the miracles of good music or good friends, even as he wanted most fervently to die. Dying wasn't antithetical to these miracles but inseparable from them. None of our joys is forever.

The elders' gift to me was a simple one: a reminder that time is both limited and really amazing, every day as momentous and quotidian as *Ulysses.* Any turn might bring hot-buttered satisfaction or a trip to the ER; the challenge is to figure out how to live on the way to the bend. So often we measure the day by what we do with it — cure cancer or surf in Maui or meet with our child's math teacher — and overlook what is truly miraculous, which is the arrival of another day. Enjoy it or not. The day doesn't care, but if you miss it, it won't be back again.

The six or seven elders were flawed teachers, and I a flawed student, but some days the wisdom sinks in. On those days I sleep peacefully and help a stranger; call an old friend or tell my partner I love her; write in joy rather than in struggle. Food tastes better. Gratitude, purpose, camaraderie, love, family, usefulness, art, pleasure — all these are within my grasp, requiring of me only that I receive them. Those days I am kinder, more patient, more productive, less anxious, possibly closer to being the person I always should have been. Maybe my angels are even helping out. Whatever aches I had, or fears, are still with me, but as supporting instruments in my soundtrack, not as the music itself. Wine helps. Get me a gin!

In *I Had Nowhere to Go,* a memoir of his uprooted years, Jonas describes standing on the deck of the USS *General R. L. Howze* with 1,341 other displaced persons as the lights of New York City came into view. To the west were the cliffs of the Palisades and the blazing neon Ferris wheel of Palisades Amusement Park; behind them the gleaming suspension cables of the George Washington Bridge. It was somewhere around 10:00 p.m. on October 29, 1949, four and a half years after the Germans surrendered to end World War II, and the people on the deck had been stateless for longer than that, some likely never to feel at home again. After twelve days at sea they were wet and cold, seasick, at the mercy of the ocean and the new world in front of them. "I am taken over by an animal fear," Jonas wrote of the journey. New York was unknowable to them, a future that held misery and unspeakable loneliness for some, indifference for many, and fulfillment (however defined) for a few. Some would be broken and never repaired. One would become Jonas Mekas. Among the things he learned on the journey was that you don't ever really arrive, but are always displaced and impermanent, hungry for both the past that you left and the future you think awaits, both illusions. "We came here," he wrote in an undated entry from 1955, "in the continuation of an old tradition of early settlers: not for the sake of a better life but as exiles, outcasts, as our only place of escape from sure death.

"No, we didn't come to the West for a better life! Nor did we come in search of adventure. We chose the West, America, from sheer instinct of survival, a survival physical and brutal."

This strikes me as a way to approach old age, or any age: as a landscape unknown and unchosen, full of uncertainty, better than the alternative. We're all on that cold transport ship, sometimes shivering and seasick, displaced from the hearth that once

306

comforted us, changed by our losses, anxious about what is to come. The bright lights glisten in front of us, the opportunities for growth or decline. Like the refugees, we have reason to be afraid: the hardships looming are as big as the land itself. But we'll arrive with whatever resourcefulness enabled us to get on that ship in the first place, bruised but resilient. In time, there will come days when that is not enough. Hips break, hearts fail, memories blur, partners exit before us.

You make your deal with that future now and renegotiate as you go along. Is it a life worth living? For how long? In the meantime, what about the minute in front of you, or the day, or the month: Is it worth living? Can you keep dancing, keep singing, have a good drink, and not get too serious? Play mah-jongg with friends, listen rapt to Sondra Radvanovsky or Jonas Kaufmann, have some ice cream, which you're not supposed to have? Yes indeedy. Eventually, of course, that life will kill you. But there will be time for that when the day comes. And a lesson of my year with the oldest old is that the years leading up to it will not be what you think.

Of course, I could be wrong about all of

307

this, in which case I will have spent all those years living more happily in vain. I can live with that.

EPILOGUE

Most people my age are dead at the present time. You could look it up.
— Casey Stengel, age seventy-two

Before I met the six people in this book, if I thought about my old age at all, I imagined it to be like my present life, only with everything good stripped away — eyesight, mobility, sex, independence, purpose, dignity. In their place I imagined constant back pain and a home that smelled funny. Maybe I would run out of money or recede into senile dementia. In 2008, I took part in a simulation called Xtreme Aging in Columbus, Ohio, developed to help health care workers understand what it's like to get old. We put on glasses to distort our vision, latex gloves and adhesive bands around our knuckles to reduce our fine motor skills, cotton in our ears and noses, and corn kernels in our shoes to simulate the pains from loss of fatty tissue. "I must say, you look lovely," the group leader told us. Then she gave us some simple tasks to perform. Count out money at a supermarket line, she said. Now try buttoning a shirt or using a cell phone. This view of old age scared me and depressed me. Often it still does.

The new year, 2016, brought a new round of challenges for the elders. Fred Jones had ended 2015 nearly homebound after the amputation of two toes, and the cold months and short days of January and February did little to motivate him to get out. His daughter's breast cancer was making its final deadly push, and his life at home was becoming precarious. One day in his apartment, he put a dinner from Meals on Wheels on the stove to warm it up, then lay down to rest a minute. "Thank God for the smoke alarm," he said. "Yes indeed." It wasn't his first such incident.

In March 2016, a few weeks before his eighty-ninth birthday, he had a dream about being in a building with no roof, with objects falling on him from above — in one telling, a chandelier; in another, melons and other fruits. The dream scared him and he fell out of bed, unable to get up. The first time he told me about the dream he seemed shaken by the vision of things falling out of the sky on him, but later he said that he thought it signified the blessings God was going to send down to him.

That was Fred. Less than a month later, his daughter died, and before she was even buried, Fred had a heart attack that took him off. "The social worker said he died of a broken heart," his granddaughter Danielle Jones said. "And it's true." Jim Healy, the man who bought Fred the purple suit and befriended him in his final year, said, "You could say he died of a three-story unheated walk-up," and this was true, too. He was the youngest of the six elders and the first to go. Fred and I never did get to Red Lobster as we had planned. But if there's an afterlife and we should meet there, the shrimp is on me. I know he'll be smiling when we meet. And I'll smile right back.

I visited John Sorensen in his apartment for the last time in March of 2016. Anne told me he had fallen several times in the new year, but John had no memory of falling. He seemed weak but as always happy to talk, more forgetful than in the past. Four times in our conversation he asked whether I had ever seen *Seven Brides for Seven Brothers* — it's really good, he said each time.

"For an old man I'm doing pretty good, I

guess," he said, surprising me. "I'm content being here. I'm having trouble with the television, but Walter's here."

He told a story about his mother giving up her house in upstate New York to move to California, where some of her relatives lived. She was old by then, and the house, which had been a tavern during the Revolutionary War, was too much for her to take care of.

"All I can tell you is that the woman who got on the plane and the woman who got off was an entirely different person," John said. "You wouldn't know it was her. My mother died that day. What was left was not my mother. All her personality was gone. I feel the same way. I can't leave this house. Because Walter's here. No he isn't, and I don't believe in an afterlife, but there are so many things that remind me of him."

Anne had often said that moving John out of the apartment would kill him, and as he grew frailer, she persuaded him to let her apply for full-time aides, which he had refused in the past. Her mission was to get Medicaid approval before it was too late. "I'm not in a great mood today, but I'm not in a real bad mood," he said. "I feel useless. I feel like a piece of garbage that should be thrown away. I can't do anything even if I wanted to do it. I guess I could still go outside but I don't want to. The sun hurts me. There's nothing for me to do. I can't do anything."

In May 2016, John collapsed in his apartment and probably lay on the floor for two days before a neighbor heard him calling out, Anne said. From the day I met him he'd said he wanted to die, and now he seemed to be on his way. His last weeks, in a hospital and then a rehab center, were filled with visits from friends and the aides and volunteers who had helped him at home. One sang his favorite arias to him; others played music on their phones. Even as he refused food, slowly starving himself to death, he thanked his nurses profusely for every kindness. "I'm never going to get better," he told one nurse, complimenting her long eyelashes. "You're pretty anyway."

In his last days, he revisited happy memories from his upstate childhood or his time with Walter on Fire Island; when his occupational therapist said he would return the next day, John told him, "I look forward to it already." He died on June 26, 2016, as ready as a person can be. Anne planned to scatter his ashes with Walter's on Fire Island, but because of scheduling conflicts, it had to wait another year.

The other four elders and my mother are still carrying on as I write in the summer of 2017, each exceeding their life expectancy with every passing day.

Helen Moses, like her beloved Mets, had an up-and-down year.

In the fall of 2016, Helen complained to the nursing home staff and to her daughter about pains in her stomach. Then, after two days, she started vomiting blood. "That's when I got scared," she said. "And when I saw it was so red, I knew I was in trouble."

She spent nearly two weeks in the intensive care unit at New York-Presbyterian Hospital, where she was treated for a bleeding ulcer and a possible blood clot on top of the ulcer.

"I thought I was not going to make it," she said. "I said, 'This is the end.' I cried a little bit. But I'm always crying anyway, so they didn't listen to me." She added, "I wasn't scared. I wasn't afraid to die."

When she returned home, weak and twenty pounds lighter, it was to the love triangle with Howie and her daughter, Zoe. Both suffered during her crisis.

Howie was lonely and barely ate while she

was away, unable to visit her in the hospital. Zoe, who visited the ICU every day, was emotionally wracked to see her mother in such a fragile condition. She even started being nicer to Howie, she said. In her mother's room in December, she teared up at the memory.

"I don't know what I'd do without her," Zoe said. "She's my funny lady. It hits me here, because it's a change."

"I won't be here forever," Helen said.

"Ma, you're going to make me cry. Yes you will."

"I don't want to be here forever anyway," Helen said.

"Don't make me cry," Zoe said. "Of course you are. What am I supposed to do without you?"

Helen recovered from her surgery and regained her roar. Being ninety-two, she said, was "the same as being ninety-one. Next year we'll probably be married." She was fearless, but she waited until her daughter was out of the room before mentioning marriage. The Mets, as of this writing, have their own problems.

Ping Wong, who had scored a golden ticket in the social services system, seemed to run out of luck. In the summer and autumn of 2016 she had a series of minor falls that landed her in the hospital and then in a nursing home for rehab.

Ping's apartment had been a cocoon that enabled her to live safely and comfortably, with some physical exercise and regular mental stimulation from her daily mah-jongg games. She had foods she liked and friends she saw every day. Routines like hers often hide the progress of cognitive decline. Away from this cocoon, her dementia either advanced or became more noticeable, and her daughter decided that it was no longer safe for her to live on her own.

The first stop, in late 2016, was a nursing home on Manhattan's Upper East Side, where few or no residents spoke Cantonese, and no one played mah-jongg. This left Ping, who thrived on social interaction, largely on her own, without even her plants to occupy her. When I visited her, she seemed uncharacteristically passive and resigned, and she was not exactly sure where she was. Friends from her old building couldn't manage the obstacles of language and transit to visit. "When you're old, everything is change change change," Ping said of her new circumstances. "Too much change. Hard for old people."

In December her daughter moved her to a nursing home near her in southern New

Jersey that had a wing with thirty-four Chinese residents. A week into her stay, I found her playing mah-jongg for the first time since she left her apartment. It was not quite like old times — the four players all spoke different dialects, and the New Jersey crowd played a slightly different version of the game than she was used to — but she was more alert and responsive, engaged in the game and conversation afterward. She was aware of her memory lapses, she said, but not too bothered by them. "From the bathroom coming out to the bedroom, I forget what I want, so I have to go back," she said. "But not so often."

I asked whether she could still make herself happy.

She thought about the question. "It's very difficult to say now," she said. "I haven't made intimate friends yet. I'm getting old. Change of place is not so good. You have to adjust yourself to new surroundings. It's not easy."

Five months later, at her ninety-second birthday, her progress remained mixed. Early in her stay at the home she had fallen, and the staff felt she was not safe on her feet, so she was now confined to a wheel-chair, and the muscles around her artificial hips knotted painfully. Her dementia also had its own way with her. One day she told her daughter to get her out of the home before Japanese soldiers killed her, a flash-back to the occupation of Hong Kong during World War II.

None of that decline was apparent during the birthday celebration. Sharing a colorful Chinatown birthday cake with a few relatives, she said she was now happy with her life there. She couldn't tend to her plants — "I'm too busy," she said — but at least she was around other Cantonese speakers. She said she hoped to make it to one hundred, but then seemed to reconsider. "My doctor, after he examined me once, said my heart was very strong. 'You will have longer life.' I said I don't want longer life. Longer life, you have to work hard."

Ruth Willig had one more special lesson for me. In the fall of 2016, her daughter Judy told me that Ruth had declined dramatically since I had last seen her. But when I visited Ruth, she seemed as resourceful and self-sufficient as ever. Her hands shook more than in the past, but she was looking forward to the birth of her first great-grandchild, planning to knit a blanket for the baby. "Judy always exaggerates," she said. "She worries about me too much, she really does. More than necessary, I'd say. I'm really okay. I've been a little down, but I have the ups, too." Around that time, during a visit with my mother, one of her friends described her in ways wholly unrecognizable to me — lighthearted, outgoing, always in good spirits. The friend chided me gently for underestimating my mother, adding that I was typical of other visiting relatives, not realizing what full lives our elders lived. A call from Helen's daughter, Zoe, similarly described Helen at death's door from the ulcer, but left out how far she had recovered since then.

So what to make of this discrepancy between the way these three older women saw their lives and the way their children saw them? The elders were leading lives that were fuller, of more value, than what we saw. Where we focused on day-to-day changes, which were almost always for the worse, they lived more in the continuities. Perhaps the best response to this disparity is simply "Duh!" Old age remains a topic on which we middle-aged people think we know it all. The three women were saying that we didn't: that from up close their lives looked different from what we saw. Even after my year with the elders, I realized, I still saw my mother's life through my prejudices about old age. The life she actually led was something else.

"I was trying to think of what I could tell you about this year," Ruth said when we got together. "Do I feel a year older? I'm ninety-three, and I tell people I'm ninety-three. I'm kind of proud of myself. 'Cause I'm still independent." It hurt her to stand up, but she walked across the room to get a bowl of chocolates. "Take a few," she said, and sat back down. "I hate getting up from the chair."

"For a while," she said, "when I reached ninety, I was excited. I thought, Okay, time to go. Now I don't know anymore. I don't strive to be a hundred like a lot of people do. The rest is a bonus."

Of the three male elders, Jonas Mekas survived the following year as jaunty and purposeful as ever. From the time we met, he was focused on organizing a benefit art auction to keep Anthology Film Archives alive. With so many old movies now available online, it was hard to get people to come to the theater. Jonas's plan was to build a café inside the theater that would pay for the Archives' other activities. He just needed six million dollars. It would probably take a year to put the auction together, he said in early 2015.

On March 2, 2017, a crowd that included John Waters, Greta Gerwig, Steve Buscemi, Jim Jarmusch, and Zosia Mamet turned out, bidding on works by Richard Serra, Cindy Sherman, Matthew Barney, Chuck Close, Christo, Ai Weiwei, and other supporters of Jonas. The designer Zac Posen bought an as-yet-unwritten song by Laurie Anderson. "I have no idea what he'll want me to write about," she said later. Patti Smith sang with R.E.M.'s Michael Stipe, changing the last line of her biggest hit to "Because the night belongs to JONAS," to big applause. The auction raised more than $2 million, with a matching pledge for another $2 million.

Jonas continued working apace, organizing his materials for books and exhibitions. After the presidential election, he did not share the gloom that settled over many people he knew. He had lived through Stalin's invasion of Lithuania and Hitler's slave labor camps; he would survive Donald Trump, he said. "I think I am optimistic, because I see everything in a longer time perspective," he said. "So okay, when all my friends are panicking about Trump, I see it as two steps forward, one step back, and that has always been — all the wise men, from Confucius as far as we know, thought that that's how humanity works. One step back may be pretty hard to take, but it's a normal thing. It'll come back again. The development of humanity can never be stopped."

In April of 2017, as Jonas planned to travel to Athens to show photos from his years in displaced persons camps, he gave an e-mail interview to a British publication called *Our Culture Mag*. The interviewer asked, "If you could give any advice to a person that wants to be [a] filmmaker, what would it be?" The response was pure Jonas. "Get a camera!"

My friend Robert Moss, who is in his eighties and still directing plays around the East Coast, once told me about a visit to his cardiologist, a droll man with a Saharan sense of humor. "I have bad news," the doctor told him after the exam. "You're going to live to a hundred." Robert was confused. "Is that bad news?" he asked. The doctor looked at him sharply. "Is that good news?" he said. Everyone's a comic.

Robert founded a successful theater company in a Times Square YMCA in 1971, and when he was asked years later how he was able to accomplish all that he has, he said, "I never thought about what would happen if it rained." In my time with the elders, I found myself coming back to these words often. They didn't mean that Robert suffered fewer hardships than other people — since he didn't pack an umbrella, he probably got rained on more than his share. But he didn't get paralyzed by things that hadn't happened yet, and he learned by necessity how much he could accomplish even when it was raining.

The elders were all proof that you could live a full and fulfilling life even when the weather turned stormy. So why worry about the clouds in the forecast? Live your life, put on a show, take a chance, give thanks for your failures along with your successes — they're two sides of the same coin. If we're living longer, maybe we have an obligation to live better: wiser, kinder, more grateful and forgiving, less vengeful and covetous. All those things make life better for everyone, but especially the person trying to live by them. Even, I would add, when we fail in our attempts to get there. As the character Dean Moriarty says in Jack Kerouac's *On the Road,* "Troubles, you see, is the generalization-word for what God exists in. The thing is not to get hung up."

The ugliness of the presidential election tested how deeply I had absorbed the lessons of this book. Whatever your political views, the raw animosities that boiled up during the campaign and after were reason to worry. Was I really able to give thanks for being plunged into that mess, to make myself happy, to avoid fruitless conflict, to accept my mortality, to live with purpose, to cultivate poetry and saints? Waking up the morning after Election Day, was I really still happy? As I write now, it is still too early to declare victory on any of these fronts. I've spent too much of my life seeing the glass as not only half empty but a crappy excuse for a glass. I can't say I'm inoculated from those doldrums and rages now.

But I've learned some things. I was surprisingly accepting of the death of John Sorensen, who wanted to go, and also of Fred, who so gamely looked for another twenty years. I liked both men, and miss them, but I wouldn't wish anyone eternal life. When a friend had a serious health crisis, I didn't fall into despair over what might happen next, as I would have in the past, but I still robustly celebrated every positive sign in his treatment. This isn't an argument for complacency. You still have to fight what you can fight. Treat your cancer, bug your doctors, take a stand, demand justice, get arrested. But you won't always win; happiness means seeing the good even in your losses.

After the election I took stock of the things that made my life worthwhile and found that all would endure, however loud people yelled on cable news. Ditto if I lost my job or shattered my pelvis; nothing would be much better if I won the lottery or developed buns of steel. Politics matter, of course, as do money and health. But they aren't the makings of a life well lived. At some point in your travels they'll probably fail you. The good things in life — happiness, purpose, contentment, companionship, beauty, and love — have been there all along. We don't need to earn them. Good food, friends, art, warmth, worth — these are the things we have already. We just need to choose them as our lives.

It's the simplest of lessons, but one I'm still steering toward. Sometimes it's not easy doing what's easy. I've spent years thinking that life's meaning lay in struggle and distrusting ease as a cop-out. Now I'm not so sure; often I wish I had those years back. But as Jonas says, if you want to be a filmmaker, get a camera! The exclamation point is his. But the joy behind it — the genius of it — is there for all of us.

New York City, June 2017

NOTES

1. Surprise of a Lifetime

"One of the few advantages of age": Penelope Lively, *Dancing Fish and Ammonites: A Memoir* (New York: Viking Penguin, 2013), 1, 8.

As May Sarton wrote: May Sarton, *As We Are Now* (New York: W. W. Norton, 1973), 23.

In one study, people over sixty said: Peter Uhlenberg and Jenny de Jong Gierveld, "Age-Segregation in Later Life: An Examination of Personal Networks," *Ageing & Society* 24 (2004): 5–28.

Older people report a greater sense of well-being: Laura L. Carstensen, Bulent Turan, Susanne Scheibe, et al., "Emotional Experience Improves with Age: Evidence Based on Over 10 Years of Experience Sampling," *Psychology and Aging* 26, no. 1 (March 2011): 21–33.

"At eighty I believe I am a far more cheerful person": Henry Miller, *Sextet* (New York: New Directions, 2010), 5.

At age eighty-five and older, 72 percent of people: All statistical breakdowns for people eighty-five and up come from the United States Census Bureau's 2009–2013 American Community Survey, with data analysis by Susan Weber-Stoger, senior research specialist and SAS programmer at Social Explorer and the CUNY Center for Advanced Technology.

2. The Paradox of Old Age

"That was the first lesson": Laura L. Carstensen, *A Long Bright Future: Happiness, Health, and Financial Security in an Age of Increased Longevity* (New York: PublicAffairs, 2009), 6.

"separate the problems of aging": Ibid., 7.

One participant, Jan Post: Stephen S. Hall, *Wisdom: From Philosophy to Neuroscience* (New York: Vintage Books, 2011), 62.

Other experiments added nuance: Laura L. Carstensen, "Growing Old or Living Long: Take Your Pick," *Issues in Science and Technology* 23, no. 2 (Winter 2007).

3. Why Older Means Wiser

In the 1980s, a Swedish sociologist named Lars Tornstam: Lars Tornstam, "Maturing into Gerotranscendence," *Journal of Transpersonal Psychology* 43, no. 2 (2011): 166–180.

Two thousand years ago, the Stoic philosopher Seneca: Lucius Seneca, *Letters from a Stoic,* letter XII.

"I often feel that death is not the enemy of life": Rabbi Joshua L. Liebman, *Peace of Mind: Insights on Human Nature That Can Change Your Life* (New York: Carol Publishing, 1994), 106.

4. Love in the Time of Lipitor

In 2010, when she pleaded guilty: Daniel Bates, "Gold-Digger, 27, Jailed for Fleecing Two Disabled Lonely Hearts Out of $110,000," *Daily Mail,* December 23, 2010.

Love, he writes: Terry Eagleton, *The Meaning of Life: A Very Short Introduction* (Oxford: Oxford University Press, 2007), 168.

5. On the Other Hand . . .

In a University of Chicago study: Linda J. Waite, Edward O. Laumann, Aniruddha

Das, and L. Philip Schumm, "Sexuality: Measures of Partnerships, Practices, Attitudes, and Problems in the National Social Life, Health, and Aging Study," *Journals of Gerontology Series B: Psychological Sciences and Social Sciences* 64B, suppl. 1 (November 2009): i56–i66.

A 2010 study by researchers at Indiana University's Center for Sexual Health Promotion: Chart online at www.nationalsexstudy.indiana.edu/graph.html.

As Laura Carstensen writes, "Bad relationships": Laura L. Carstensen, *A Long Bright Future: Happiness, Health, and Financial Security in an Age of Increased Longevity* (New York: PublicAffairs, 2009), 108.

But when the psychologists: Howard S. Friedman and Leslie R. Martin, *The Longevity Project: Surprising Discoveries for Health and Long Life from the Landmark Eight-Decade Study* (New York: Hudson Street Press, 2011), 180.

6. More Years, Less Life?

"Instead of enhancing the people's health": Ernest M. Gruenberg, "The Failures of Success," *Milbank Memorial Fund Quarterly: Health and Society* 55, no. 1 (Winter

1977): 3–24.

In a widely circulated essay: Ezekiel J. Emanuel, "Why I Hope to Die at 75," *The Atlantic,* October 2014.

The geriatrician Bill Thomas: Bill Thomas, *Second Wind: Navigating the Passage to a Slower, Deeper, and More Connected Life* (New York: Simon & Schuster, 2014), 130.

a Stanford rheumatologist named James F. Fries: James F. Fries, "The Compression of Morbidity," *Milbank Quarterly* 83, no. 4 (December 2005): 801–823.

"It is time to stop thinking about": Elkhonon Goldberg, *The Wisdom Paradox: How Your Mind Can Grow Stronger as Your Brain Grows Older* (New York: Pocket Books, 2007), 18.

7. The Lessons of Fred

G. K. Chesterton wrote that "thanks are the highest form": Gilbert Keith Chesterton, *A Short History of England* (U.S.: Renaissance Classics, 2012), 43.

"before the play and the opera": Quoted by Catholic G. K. Chesterton Society, www .catholicgkchestertonsociety.co.uk.

In 2015, researchers at the University of Southern California: Glenn R. Fox, Jonas Kaplan, Hanna Damasio, and Antonio

Damasio, "Neural Correlates of Gratitude," *Frontiers in Psychology* 6 (September 2015), article 1491.

Back in 2003, he and Michael E. McCullough: Robert A. Emmons and Michael E. McCullough, "Counting Blessings Versus Burdens: An Experimental Investigation of Gratitude and Subjective Well-Being in Daily Life," *Journal of Personality and Social Psychology* 84 (2003): 377–389.

8. The Lessons of Ping

A few years ago, a group of elderly Korean gardeners: Derek Kravitz, "Dispute Grows Tense Over Community Garden in Queens," *Wall Street Journal,* August 1, 2013.

In another incident, police were called: Sarah Maslin Nir and Jiha Ham, "Korean Community Leaders Urge McDonald's Boycott," *New York Times,* January 16, 2014.

A 2013 study conducted by the Center for an Urban Future: Christian González-Rivera, "The New Face of New York's Seniors," available at https://nycfuture.org/pdf/The-New-Face-of-New-Yorks-Seniors.pdf.

Karl Pillemer of Cornell makes the distinction: Karl Pillemer, *30 Lessons for Living: Tried and True Advice from the Wisest Americans*

(New York: Plume, 2012), 163.

In 1993 and 1994, researchers at four university medical centers: Joel Tsevat, Neal V. Dawson, Albert W. Wu, et al., "Health Values of Hospitalized Patients 80 Years or Older," *Journal of the American Medical Association* 279, no. 5 (February 4, 1998): 371–375.

Even people with dementia: Toby Williamson, "My Name Is Not Dementia: People with Dementia Discuss Quality of Life Indicators," published by the Alzheimer's Society (UK), 2010.

9. The Lessons of John

"pioneers in a land where": Deepak Chopra, *The Essential Ageless Body, Timeless Mind: The Essence of the Quantum Alternative to Growing Old* (New York: Harmony Books, 2007), 11.

The psychologist Mary Pipher: Mary Pipher, *Another Country: Navigating the Emotional Terrain of Our Elders* (New York: Riverhead Books, 1999), 15–16.

Unpaid caregivers provide 90 percent: "Family Caregiving: The Facts," Centers for Disease Control fact sheet, available at www.cdc.gov/aging/caregiving/facts.htm.

A 2014 study by the RAND Corporation:

Amalavoyal V. Chari, John Engberg, Kristin Ray, and Ateev Mehrotra, *Valuing the Care We Provide Our Elders* (Santa Monica, CA: RAND Corporation, 2015), available at www.rand.org/pubs/research_briefs/RB9817.html.

The National Institutes of Health warn: Richard Schulz and Paula R. Sherwood, "Physical and Mental Health Effects of Family Caregiving," *American Journal of Nursing* 108, no. 9, supplement (September 2008): 23–27.

10. The Lessons of Helen

Nursing facilities like the Hebrew Home: Sidney D. Watson, "From Almshouses to Nursing Homes and Community Care: Lessons from Medicaid's History," *Georgia State University Law Review* 26, no. 3 (2009), article 13.

By December 31, 2014: CMS Nursing Home Data Compendium, 2015, www.cms.gov/Medicare/Provider-Enrollment-and-Certification/CertificationandCompliance/Downloads/nursinghomedatacompendium_508-2015.pdf.

11. The Lessons of Ruth

"Receiving is much harder than giving": Wendy Lustbader, "The Dilemmas of Dependency," *Journal of Case Management* 4, no. 4: 132–135.

"The reward for recognizing resentment": Wendy Lustbader, *Counting on Kindness: The Dilemmas of Dependency* (New York: Free Press, 1991), 26.

12. The Lessons of Jonas

He once counted the village population: Jonas Mekas, *I Had Nowhere to Go* (Newfane, VT: New Thistle Press, 1991), 1.

His best-known poems: Jonas Mekas, *Idylls of Semeniskiai* (Annandale, NY: Hallelujah Editions, 2007), 2.

Studies with Danish twins: Robert N. Butler, *The Longevity Revolution: The Benefits and Challenges of Living a Long Life* (New York: PublicAffairs, 2008), 91.

In one study, those who had more positive views: Becca R. Levy, Martin D. Slade, Terrence E. Murphy, and Thomas M. Gill, "Association Between Positive Age Stereotypes and Recovery from Disability in Older Persons," *Journal of the American Medical Association* 308, no. 19 (November 21, 2012): 1972–1973.

As the filmmaker Stan Brakhage: Calvin Tompkins, "All Pockets Open," *The New Yorker,* January 6, 1973, 31–49.

The neurologist Oliver Sacks: Oliver Sacks, "My Own Life: Oliver Sacks on Learning He Has Terminal Cancer," *New York Times,* February 19, 2015.

"I am taken over by an animal fear": Mekas, *I Had Nowhere to Go,* 288.

"We came here": Ibid., 461.

ACKNOWLEDGMENTS

Since this book is in part about the value of gratitude, I offer this page less as obligatory back matter and more as the big finish. Cue the fireworks and confetti; the bar is open.

My greatest thanks go to the six elders and their families who opened their lives to me, always receiving me with generosity and candor, even on days when they might not have felt up to it. Special thanks to Judy Willig, Zoe Gussoff, Anne Kornblum, Sebastian Mekas, and Elaine Gin for sharing both their loved ones and their wisdom with me.

To my mother, of course, my gratitude is beyond measure, and still not enough. Don't get me started.

Several editors at *The New York Times* made the project possible. Amy Virshup and I spent more than a year turning over different strategies for how best to cover the oldest old before arriving at the simplest:

Pick some people and see how they live; let their lives be the story. Newspaper series typically require sharper focus than that, and I credit Amy for giving me time and leeway to pursue something so open-ended. Who knew the six people would prove so interesting? Amy did, that's who. Amy, Jan Benzel, and Bill Ferguson edited the articles and helped me absorb the lessons in this book, and Wendell Jamieson, the *Times*'s metro editor, gave his blessing and unflagging support. Ace photographer Nicole Bengiveno was my partner throughout, as curious about our subjects' lives as I was. We played good cop/better cop.

Sarah Crichton helped shape this book long before she became its masterful editor. I've been grateful for her smarts and faith and friendship since she hired me at *Newsweek* in 1991, and the debt keeps getting deeper and sweeter. Paul Bresnick, my agent, nudged the book along from wishful thinking to finished manuscript.

John Capouya, Drew Keller, and Caren Browning all provided invaluable help with the manuscript.

ABOUT THE AUTHOR

John Leland is a reporter at *The New York Times,* where he wrote a yearlong series that became the basis for *Happiness Is a Choice You Make,* and the author of two previous books, *Hip: The History* and *Why Kerouac Matters: The Lessons of "On the Road" (They're Not What You Think).* Before joining the *Times,* he was a senior editor at *Newsweek,* editor in chief of *Details,* a reporter at *Newsday,* and a writer and editor at *Spin* magazine.